IN THE WARMTH OF THE SHADOW

ROBERT N. RUESCH

D1403433

Psalm 45:1

ISBN 978-1-64028-534-7 (Paperback)
ISBN 978-1-64028-535-4 (Digital)

Christian Faith Publishing, Inc.
296 Chestnut Street
Meadville, PA 16335
www.christianfaithpublishing.com

Photographs are the property of the YMCA of the Rockies, Lula W. Dorsey Museum, unless otherwise noted.

Printed in the United States of America

CONTENTS

ENDORSEMENTS

Robert Ruesch offers a rare window into the wonderful world of adoption I know firsthand. He gives all the credit to God who led him to Walter and Alice Ruesch and the rest of his extended adopted family at the YMCA of the Rockies! You can't help but bask 'In the Warmth of the Shadow' reliving his remarkable childhood memories thanks to a love that knows no bounds! – *Stephanie Riggs - Journalist*

In the Warmth of the Shadow is a celebration of family and faith. I am grateful that Bob shared his memories with me, and that the Lula W Dorsey Museum at the YMCA of the Rockies could contribute photographs and research support throughout Bob's project. As the Historian for the YMCA of the Rockies, I recommend In the Warmth of the Shadow to anyone interested in truly understanding the depth to which time at the YMCA of the Rockies can impact ones' life. From a single summer visit to a lifetime of return trips, Bob captured the spirit of the YMCA of the Rockies through story. Thank you for sharing Bob! – *Carie Essig, Association Historian and Museums Director, YMCA of the Rockies*

DEDICATED TO

Walter & Alice Ruesch, and those who worked at the YMCA of the Rockies helping to define what a family experience can really be. And to my family for listening more than once to the memories of my childhood.

PART I

THOUGHTS

CHAPTER ONE

PRELUDE

Someone said, "Every book you've ever read is just a different combination of twenty-six letters." Words are also like the notes in music. There is a medley, and you just have to write things down using the twenty-six letters and the tune you hear in your soul. It often does not matter what is inscribed on a page; the process of writing is the calling. If you would as a "writer," why then do they write, and there would be as many answers as there are people who communicate in the form of words on paper.

My specific reason for writing is to glorify God. Simple, and as easy and difficult as that. This journey of pen to paper is one that started many years ago and never was answered. Now the time is right because of a contest with NaNoWriMo (the National Novel Writing Month), which came as a challenge from a friend that wanted an accountability partner in the time frame of thirty days to complete a novel of fifty thousand words. Only 11 percent finished the task. We are in the 11 percent.

I grew up in a resort world of opportunity where families, conferences, and college students from all over the United States traveled to the Colorado Rockies to gather, meet, and work. What a cauldron of learning for a Wisconsin-born child to learn about many subjects over a summertime of growing up from the age of five to twenty.

These are the thoughts, stories, memories of a boy in a vacation world. Perhaps some of the facts are not just right, but the reality is, this is what is remembered. Time has been taken to get the history of the YMCA of the Rockies (known in the 1950s as Association Camp) right. If I missed a historical truth, I apologize. However, the reason for the walk (sometimes run) down memory lane is because, I believe, God has called me to write, and thus I will. Also, when you are asked to account to another writer and agree, you commit to the process.

A successful writer friend of mine has a term, "Life is an adventure created by God." I could not agree more.

So, dear reader, travel with me, the memories, the anecdotes, and past times of a boy learning about the adventure of life one summer week at a time, watching his father take a seasonal regional mountaintop camp and transform the place into a world-recognized world-class resort where people's lives are changed forever.

Being in the warmth of the shadow was an honor. I didn't realize it at the time, but I do now, and I hope you see that in this "based on a true story" novel.

God bless. I know He has blessed my life.

CHAPTER TWO

THANKS

Give thanks in all circumstances;
for this is God's will for you in Christ Jesus.
—1 Thessalonians 5:18

Bob Hope famously said, "Thanks for the memories." This was his signature line, but is it not everyone's? All our lives are a savings bank of memories; some are good, others not so good, but memories all the same.

I was blessed by God's plan to be adopted by Walter and Alice Ruesch, who for many years tried unsuccessfully to have natural children. Eventually, the family doctor said, the next time, Mom would not survive childbirth, but the baby might. That was when they decided to adopt a little blond eight-month-old baby born in Oshkosh, Wisconsin, home of the Green Bay Packers.

There is an interesting side story. Dad played for the team that became the Green Bay Packers. He was the semi-truck offensive and defensive center weighing in at 380 pounds. He was paid $25 for a home game and $50 for an away game, good money back then.

My very first memory, verified by my mother, was me being handed from the nurse to my dad and seeing what I know now as his car out the second-story window of the adoption agency.

They, whoever "they" are, say babies can't remember that early. I beg to differ. I knew at that instant I was part of a family, not a crying baby in the newborn section of the hospital attended by the nursing staff.

Our family journey to Association Camp, as the YMCA of the Rockies was called in the 1950's was from Wisconsin, to summer youth camps in Kansas and Nebraska and then in October of 1950, a visit to Estes Park and a winter's job offer for the role of director at the Y camp.

From that point, this person's life at the age of five started. I had a whole camp to roam and wander as I grew up. What an opportunity to explore all summer the nooks and crannies of a camp where "you could throw a cat through the outer wall and not scare the cat," according to Dad when he took over the leadership of a seasonal summer camp.

Many of the memories I had were formed in the snippet of time I was with my father as the operation of the Y camp was conducted. His job was 24-7 and had to be if the goals he set were to be accomplished. Family was primary to him as well as work. Looking back now at my time in my life as a grandfather, father, and retired individual, I don't know how he managed all he did. He was out early in the morning, and late in the evening he would come home. Sometimes the only opportunity to see him was in his office or at the staff dining room.

We would host many divergent people in our summer home, one of them was Dr. Peter Drucker, author, speaker, professor at Stanford University. I have in our library a book on nonprofit management signed to my father by Dr. Drucker, which states, "To Walt, a person who knows more about managing nonprofits than I could ever write in a book."

Tom Landry, head coach of the Dallas Cowboys for many years, and James Jeffery, one of the founders of the Fellowship of Christian Athletes both graced our summer home, along with many others. They would just come by, sit, and talk.

However, my memories come more from the staff and the summer employees who shaped a part of my life. The opportunity to hang around college students in the summer presented opportunities to learn things at an accelerated rate. I learned to play bridge in sev-

IN THE WARMTH OF THE SHADOW

enth grade. I had read *Atlas Shrugged* by Ayn Rand before I was in high school. I learned about colleges and universities across the USA from an early age. I knew what "hook 'em horns" meant in junior high and "roll tide."

The full-time staff provided ages of guidance for me when I could not understand the why of something. They were the extended family of support that many times brought into focus the understanding of a process or situation, even when tragedy struck the staff or one of the guests.

Guests were a weekly or biweekly change. I made friends quickly as they came and went back to their homes in states far away. If there was an underside of growing up in a resort setting, the quick hellos and good-byes could be said to be that. I learned to not understand commitments, often of more than one to two weeks. I could not understand what all the emotion was about when people departed. To me, that was just a way of life. Didn't everyone else experience on-and-then-off relationships?

As I recall the memories of growing up at the Y camp, I am thankful for the foresight of a biological mother who recognized before childbirth the painful decision to place me for adoption. What a heart-wrenching decision for a mom to make, but the right one. Single moms in the 1940s would have more than a hard time to provide for a baby.

The circle was completed when I met my biological mom when I was fifty years old, and I was able to share with her how I had turned out. Her greatest compliment was when she asked me to tell my adoptive mom thanks for taking such great care of me.

What child cannot have a great childhood being raised in the Colorado Rockies at a resort facility and meeting hundreds of people? Everyone has opportunities, and from those opportunities, memories are created, sealed in your heart, and recalled at appropriate and sometimes awkward times in your life.

Bob Hope was right. Being thankful for the memories is a good thing; the happy and the sad, the good and the bad shape who we are. So, dear reader, these are the memories of a child raised in a vacation setting, learning to love quickly but to say good-bye even faster.

I hope you will enjoy the journey. I know I am enjoying continuing making memories and reliving a childhood blessed by God's plan.

PART II

1950–1955

CHAPTER THREE

REC ROOM AND
OLD FACEFUL

Jesus answered her, "If you knew the gift of God and who it is that asks you for a drink, you would have asked him and he would have given you living water."

—John 4:10

There are some things in life that continue to be entertaining time and time again. A drinking fountain with a mind of its own falls into this category.

Old Faceful is strategically located in the employees' rec hall in an area where the procedure of taking a sip, washing the face, or sometimes a mini-shower can be observed by almost everyone in the hall.

The Rec Hall around 1955. Summer employees were housed in the Mummy Quad, a four-building setting behind the Recreation Hall.

The rec hall is a long rectangular building with a fireplace at each end and a devilish water fountain in the middle of the north wall. When not working, summer employees gather here for bridge, reading, talking, and waiting for some unsuspecting thirsty soul to access Old Faceful. Each event is witnessed by several employees.

One would think that something as simple as getting a drink out of a fountain would not offer any entertainment and would provide refreshment only. Old Faceful was a fountain of funny occurrences, time and time again. There was even a sign over the water fountain stating its name. No one ever seemed to read the sign, until it was too late.

Sometimes the drinking fountain would be normal, and that was the way for several days. You would develop a trust that all things were good and the drinking fountain was like any other water device. Trust like that would be folly because Old Faceful would change and destroy any sense of normalcy for you one spurt at a time.

Colorado summers are dry and hot. Coming from work to the rec hall was a natural migration of staff, and needing liquid refreshment was part of that procedure.

As one came in to the rec hall, there was the fountain, holding cool liquid refreshment. You approach the fountain with the faith of a dry mustard seed, bending over, opening your mouth, and turning the handle. Then it happens—Old Faceful strikes. *Splat,* and you are bathed in the beauty of cool refreshing water—and the incident observed by the card-playing, guitar-strumming, and highly observant summer employees, who by default have been waiting for such an incident as this.

Your face is drenched, your ego cooled, and your hearing bombarded by the cheering of your fellow employees as you have now been inducted maybe for the first or countless times into the Club of Old Faceful.

Perhaps a bow is required here; definitely a towel is needed. And once again the memory of this summer is gilded into your personal history.

Now you wait, wait with the knowledge that some unsuspecting soul will be coming into the rec hall, tired and thirsty, looking for a refreshing sip of Colorado water, and instead will be rewarded with an aggressive stream from Old Faceful.

If there is a lesson to be learned from a drinking fountain in an employees' rec hall, it is simply this: in life there are choices, and deciding how you will react can catch you full in the face. How you respond to the situation is your choice.

Old Faceful is a good teacher of the unexpected.

CHAPTER FOUR

SUNDAY HYMN SING

Shout for joy to the Lord, all the earth. Worship the Lord with gladness; come before him with joyful songs. Know that the Lord is God. It is he who made us, and we are his; we are his people, the sheep of his pasture.

—*Psalm 100:1-3*

Many journeys produce unexpected memories at unique times, if one recognizes the possibility that presents itself. Sunday evening hymn sing in the Ad Building was one example of a time like that.

Back in the 1950s automobile air-conditioning was not an option on the average family vehicle. If you wanted to be cooler, you would roll down the window and open the driver or passenger wing vent, a small triangular window that could direct a small hurricane breeze of outside air against you. Other options were sleeveless shirts, shorts, and cool water, which had stop requirements of its own. With any decision, you were still hot as your family traveled from warm-weather states to the beckoning cool climate of the Colorado Rockies and the Y camp. You were willing to endure the oven-like conditions of traveling to appreciate the lower temperatures and dry air of the Mile-High State.

Traveling in the mid-fifties didn't offer other amenities of vehicles that transport families with the opportunities to watch movies, listen to personal music, or read a Kindle book. There were radio stations, but across the plains of Kansas, Nebraska, Oklahoma, and Texas, the stations would often fade away about the time you heard your favorite song. Conversation was always an option, and siblings continued to have the option of the "He touched me" and "Are we there yet?" games.

Many families would start their journey at night to have some opportunity of a cooler ride; the bonus was the children would be tucked in, asleep in the back seat of the car or station wagon. At least part of the traveling would be a little less stressful.

The excitement of travel would soon wear off as the hours wore on. Mom would have some temperature-appropriate snacks available. Bathroom breaks were at every gas stop and oftentimes at various rest stops under the shade of an occasional tree. Picnics were generally the lunchtime nourishment of choice.

Sometime in the mid to late afternoon, the Colorado Rockies would present themselves in the horizon. This sighting was a landmark blessing signaling that the arduous journey with your brothers and sisters, not to mention your parents, was soon coming to an end and the long awaited vacation would be started as the auto trip was coming to an end. If ever there was a time to thank Jesus, seeing the Colorado Rockies was one such time. Moods would be instantly lifted up with each mile that you gained altitude and the outside temperature and humidity lowered as you traveled.

Yet as journeys are just that, a journey, opportunities for surprises were there. Most roads that were traveled were, for the most part, straight with minimal curves. If one was prone to car sickness, a straight road as opposed to a mountain continually curving road was a time for the queasy stomach to protest and at the coming end of the trip.

By now, your father was tired, worn out from driving as it was his sacred duty to direct the vehicle and generally nobody else's job. Now, you were on the last curvy legs of reaching the Y camp. Nerves and attitudes were sometimes lost back at the Colorado border. The last miles were slower in speed and in emotional time.

Temperatures were cooler, attitudes were a bit warmer, yet this travel experience was part of the definition of family. Family you were. Automobile bingo had been played to the extreme, a book read that was not long enough for the trip, and an end in sight.

Finally, you and family turned into the entrance to the Y. A large sign hung over the entrance stating you were now on the land of vacation, and the good times of crafts, horseback riding, hiking, and other anticipated activities were about to begin.

Vacations come with surprises; it is a hidden rule of the experience. One surprise was about to present itself as it did with each family that arrived early evening on a Sunday, which was the usual check-in day.

As you parked the car, now known as the hot rolling metal torture chamber in your mind, you could see the majesty of the mountains directly ahead. The vast open field in front of you offered basketball, volleyball, and other opportunities to explore. Maybe your parents' mood would be better for the day of travel that started in the dark of the night and would now reflect the softening of Sunday night. All you wanted to do now was to get to your cabin that had been talked about, get the top bunk, and claim your temporary Colorado space.

The familiar sound of hymns drifted across the parking lot and increased in volume as you and your family walked up the steps to the Ad Building, where Dad would register and check in. Weary as family travelers were, the noteworthy sounds of Sunday hymns calmed the soul. Travelers from the pioneer days would have taken months to reach this destination, and your family achieved the same goal in a day.

Somehow you started to realize this as Mom took you to a chair in the lobby, gave you a hymnal, and you joined in with other weary travelers singing songs that threaded you together. Familiar verses drifted across the now finished emotional miles of your journey. "How Great Thou Art." Well-defined hymn, just look around at the scenery. "Holy, Holy, Holy." Yes, you could see that here in the sanctuary of peaks that stretched to the sky and were beckoning to be climbed. Your emotions traveled to the familiar verses of hymn after hymn, and because it was a hymn sing, all verses didn't require to be sung, and the other bonus, you could offer up a choice of your own. You didn't have to be an adult to do this. You learned this rule of opportunity quickly and started looking for your favorite hymn as you sang the last verse.

An instant congregation was placed together of families from familiar states you had traveled through to arrive at this expressed point in time. This was a God thing, to be together, joined by note after note after verse and hymn. In your excitement you noticed Dad had joined the instant choir of congregation, and he and Mom lifted their voices in a volume not generally used at your church. This prompted you to do the same, and a choir of family was formed.

There was something special, not magical, but special here, now singing at the beginning of your vacation. This was part of the journey, but at this singing juncture you found emotional gold.

You looked at the song leader, a large woman with a limp for a walk, with a voice that required no amplification and a talent to bring every key of the baby grand piano into play hymn after hymn. You realized you didn't often hear this type of music in your church back home as the dueling piano and organ guided you through each hymn selected for the service. This was different, unique, and something you and the people around you didn't want to end.

The staff at the front desk would join in when there was a break in families checking in. In a sense you felt this time was establishing your mountain family for the week you were here. It didn't matter your denomination. What mattered was your instant musical love for the people around you that you didn't know but were part of this choir on the mountaintop.

Maybe being this high up, you were closer to God, like Moses when he went to the summit of the mountain. Closer here in the clean, crisp air of Colorado. The clarity of your Christian conviction seemed more apparent here, in a building you have never been in, with people you didn't know singing hymns you all were familiar with. The long, hot, sometimes sibling-irritating trip was worth it, even if this was the only experience you would have had. Yet you knew there was more, much more to come. There were seven days of a lifetime of memories to be discovered, created, and shared in the lifetime before you.

Somehow singing together the spirit-filled words, listening to those beside you raise their voices, the piano pounding out note after note, all this combined together told you this was a memory to be cherished.

The hymn sing was winding down, and the Y camp hymn was sung, "God Who Touches Earth with Beauty." You knew this cadence of notes and words held a special place in the song leader's heart and now set the foundation in your heart for you too.

As you sang the familiar verses, they rolled across you heart like a blanket on a cold night, heating your soul in a way you never had heard the words before.

God, who touchest earth with beauty, Make me lovely too;
With Thy Spirit recreate me, Make my heart anew.

Like Thy springs and running waters, Make me crystal pure;
Like Thy rocks of towering grandeur, Make me strong and sure.

Like Thy shining waves in sunlight, Make me glad and free;
Like the straightness of the pine trees, Let me upright be.

Like the arching of the heavens, Lift my thoughts above;
Turn my dreams to noble action, Ministries of love.

God, who touchest earth with beauty, Make me lovely too;
Keep me ever, by Thy Spirit, Pure and strong and true.
(Mary S. Edgar)

Every word in the verses set a family tone for vacation. This leisure time was going to be memory special. Even at your adolescent age, you knew this week, starting now, was going to be life changing.

It was time to go to your cabin, your home away from home, the place you were wanting to get to quickly when you arrived, now seemed lower on the immediate goal listing.

Something happened within the notes in the lobby of the building with people you didn't know. Something loving in Christian theology. Perhaps when you are up in the mountains, you are closer to God. All you knew was that arriving here, singing familiar hymns next to unfamiliar people, created a thin space between heaven and earth, and you were changed, one note at a time.

CHAPTER FIVE

DISH BREAKING

*Those who guard their mouths and their tongues
keep themselves from calamity.*
                                                        —*Proverbs 21:23*

When you break something, oftentimes the item cannot be repaired. This is the case with heavy porcelain dishes. When dropped, they shatter into pieces, and there is nothing to do but clean up the mess and move on. But a seven-year-old who has been taught by his father to not drop or break things, especially dishes that you will eat from, the breaking of dishes is opposite of adult instruction.

Being seven is an impressionable age, and seeing a parental rule cast off with a crash of a dish and then another and another will burst your world of education.

At the end of the summer, close to Labor Day, there is a farewell banquet for the summer employees who now continue on with their college education. This banquet is a much touted, talked-about, and anticipated event as it is announced at the beginning of summer in staff orientation. Staff dressed up in their finest clothes, hair sprayed and styled, faces shaved, even to the point that everyone even smelled like the current manly or womanly fragrance. This was an event to not miss as you would see people you worked with—probably for the first time—in their best Sunday or go-to-meeting clothes.

Dad would dress in a suit, generally the only time in the summer, Mom in a special dress, and I was decked out in new jeans and a nice shirt. The dining hall was decorated, tablecloths were on the table, linen napkins folded, and camp silverware was even polished. No water spots this time!

The kitchen crew would serve the best meal of the summer, preparing it with care and pride. This was the final staff meal as many would be leaving after the farewell banquet.

The conference dining room opened at a specified time, not the employee dining room this time, not for the farewells, the final speeches from department heads, staff president's closing remarks, and of course, "Walt's final thoughts." That is where things started going south.

I had noticed as we sat in our designated place, not at the head table, but at the back part of the dining hall, there was a stack of those porcelain plates under the table. I called that to Dad's attention, and I was told to not worry about them.

Dinner was a feast, prime rib with all the great fixings and a dessert to die for. Then the reminiscent speeches about how great the summer was, how the summer was a success because of the staff working together as a team. It was a night for an impressionable seven-year-old to remember, but that is not all that I remembered and definitely not the focal point of the evening.

It was time for Walt's final thoughts. He stood up, towering high in his suit, shoes polished, and necktie perfectly placed. I was proud to be sitting with him, proud because he asked me and excited because I didn't get to be with him all that much at meals and this was the best time to be there beside him.

Mom moved back a few feet, which I thought interesting, as well as a few other staff members, then my chair was pulled back. Strange, I thought, but accepted the new placement.

The speech started out thanking staff for their summer service, mentioning the many states, colleges, and universities represented with summer staff. Numbers were quoted as to how many guests in conferences and families were served. Heard this before in the seasons previous.

Then the unthinkable started to happen. Dad picked up a plate and started talking about how there were things that went on in the summer that wasn't right, matter of fact, just wrong. He raised the plate and, with a downward swing of gravitational authority, smashed it on the floor.

The staff collectively stopped breathing. Walt never did things like this. He went on about other issues of consequence, and each time up went a plate and down came the object only to be smashed on the floor. After several of these incidences, it was my turn to let go of the pent-up anguish of a child seeing a parent lose it and started breaking things, and in front of staff. Never had I witnessed this. Mom just sat there; the rest of the staff, as far as I was concerned, were catatonic.

I let out a wail that would have impressed any professional mourner, and I didn't quit, tears, crying, more tears; the emotional flow didn't stop. What made it worse was the laughter from people around me and the staff. Then, looking at my father, the breaker of precious plates, smiling, I took the emotion to a higher level.

At this point life as I knew it was destroyed, but there was hope as one of the older lady staff members escorted me out of the destructive room and from the farewell dinner of which I didn't want to have anything to do with anymore.

We went to the Administration Building, sat by the fire, and watched the flames, which were multicolored. She talked and told me the destruction was supposed to happen and Dad was kidding around with staff and the dishes were to be destroyed anyway because of chips in the porcelain and could not be used. That seemed to ease my soul somewhat.

After a time, the emotional outburst gave way to ice cream and chocolate. I reasoned the world would still turn on its axis and Dad was the man I thought him to be.

However, the plate smashing was never again on the farewell banquet agenda. I guess my outburst solved that.

CHAPTER SIX

FAREWELL DISH WASHING

A friend loves at all times.
—Proverbs 17:17

When the farewell banquet is over, cleanup is started. All summer the kitchen crew has prepared, served the food, and cleaned up the dining hall and done the dishes. That is not the case now. They will supervise as other staff will give back this small thanks of a summer of appreciation.

Many of the staff have not been in the massive kitchen, and the dishwasher machine is a stainless steel monster to contend with. Tonight, new staff for the first and last time will have the privilege to do the dishes.

Because staff were dressed in their finest clothes, aprons were furnished by the kitchen staff. The department heads and summer staff now will give back to those who cooked, scrubbed the pots and cleaned the dining room as a gesture of gratitude for a summer of meals. A new skill will be learned, and there will be more people helping to make the chore quick and easy.

Aprons dawned, gloves on, and high heels off (barefoot was generally not an accepted practice in the kitchen, but on the last day, are you really going to get fired?). Dishwasher at the ready and go. There were piles of plates, stacks of saucers, containers of silverware, and loads of coffee cups and water glasses. Not to mention pitchers that held iced tea. The task seemed daunting, but those who were not at the dishwasher listening to its grinding sounds of cleaning were preparing dishes for washing or taking the hot items out and stacking them.

We knew this was the last time we would be together as a staff. We knew as soon as you got into your car or whomever you were hitching a ride with, the summer would be over, and the memories of what the summer was were now just that, memories. Times to be remembered, something that didn't just happen over the summer high in the Colorado Rockies, but everything that transpired in your summer now was at its end. It was fitting the final task was to clean others dishes, stack cups, and sort silverware. Somehow this was a fitting task as you were all dressed up doing a meaningful and menial task.

You didn't talk too much; talking was complete as was the summer. You were held in a close embrace of your personal thoughts of what was and what would be your future in studies.

As quick as the task of cleaning, washing, stacking, and sorting was done, you realized the summer now was really over. Work schedules done, memories placed with the plates, summer concerts over, lounging in the employees' rec hall complete.

You walked back to the rec hall with other staff, empty now of college banners, people playing bridge, the record player quiet. Old Faceful was still there, one more try, worked regular this time like it too knew the summer was closed, this chapter completed.

You had packed the staff photo of everyone and your department picture carefully as to preserve a split second of everyone's summer. Your photos were safely tucked away to show those at school what you did for the summer. They would not understand, but your memory would be recalled, and you, if only for an instant, would be transported back in time.

Hugs were distributed like candy at a holiday; tears of happiness and sometimes regret flowed. Luggage was stuffed into cars, and in the dark of the night for several hours you watched as the taillights faded, each one carrying people you loved for an instant and forever disappeared to the next phase of their life.

It was your time to go. All you had to do was go home, to your summer home. Tomorrow the employee dining room would be a ghost dining room. You would not have to wait in line. It would be quiet except for the memories whirling around in your mind. The rec hall was now a cavern. You turned out the lights and listened to the sound of crunching rocks under your feet as you too closed your summer out. This was not the first summer you have been a part of the process and would not be the last, and none of them would be easier. In some ways they became more emotional. Time creates a greater depth of commitment.

The chores were done. The staff just about gone. Tomorrow you would go back to the rec hall and listen to the silent voices of a summer past. You can sit anywhere. There is nobody home anymore; they are at or going to their homes many, many miles away.

Letters might be delivered, but probably not; college studies and other educational activities will hoard the time. Memories will be the precious jewel you will keep from that time on.

Done, finished, over, complete, lonely, not sad, it was a summer to cherish and remember. A summer of strangers working together as a team learning to care for each other, experiencing life on a mountain, close to each other, close to God, closer to who you are. A summer of discovery.

CHAPTER SEVEN

DINNER AT PATTON COURT

Bless the Lord, oh my soul and forget not all his benefits.

—Psalm 103:2

When the Y was in winter operation in the 1950s, there were only a few full-time staff on the grounds. The place was void of all the components that created what you would call "camp." If there was a working definition of a seasonal ghost town, the camp was just that in the winter months. Wind, snow, more wind, and a solitude was simply the way it was.

The town of Estes Park was basically void of population. Stores closed their doors by noon on Labor Day and would start to open on Memorial Day. It is said you could shoot a cannon down Estes's main street on Labor Day, and it would be reported by Thanksgiving, looked into by Christmas, and forgotten by Easter.

You knew winter was here because the town turned off the only stoplight and bagged it in burlap.

Dad would travel twice a week to Estes and be home in time for dinner. That was important to him to be with family at mealtime because in the summer that didn't happen often.

We lived on South Patton Court in Denver, and during the winters, the Estes staff would come down for dinner. Mom would fuss over for the week before, ever changing the menu and worrying about what was going to be. I never recall any of the meals being a disaster. But that didn't faze the unshakable Alice Ruesch. Everything needed to be perfect.

The safest offering was a pot roast. It could keep if people were late. Coming to Denver meant errands and schedules could go askew, so dinner was adjusted from the usual 5:45 time to later, which meant a snack was given to a growing boy's hungry, growling stomach.

This was a time of just fun. Little, if any, business was discussed. Mainly the topic of sports was discussed by Dad and the men. Mom and the women would talk about anything that came to mind. Sometimes the noise was a constant chatter around the dinner table.

About every week there was staff, family or guests that were invited to dinner at our home on South Patton Court in Denver. The conversations were lively and the meals well prepared by mom. Formal dinnerware was used and desert always served. Author's photo

35

It was a time of talk, tales, and the opportunity of fellowship. Dad saw the staff as equals in all areas, and having full-time, part-time, and summer staff over for dinner, coffee, or just to talk was an opportunity to learn more and appreciate to a greater depth the people he worked with.

"Walt, can you pass the rolls?" was the question posed by Roxie. You really don't say that to a person who was given scholarships to play football in college and expect to not get an athletic response. Dad did pass the roll, one of them on a high trajectory directly to Roxie. Not missing a beat, Roxie thanked Dad for the roll and said, "Now, please send the butter around." I think she feared a repeat of the first request.

While the roll was airborne, conversation ceased. Mom was ready to exit society as she knew it. Fine china, good silverware, and then food in the air was a bit over the top for her. Roxie's husband sat there, stoic, and commented, finally, "Good catch."

I, on the other hand, now recognized a new and forever family tradition of the philosophical doctrine art of roll passing. To say the least, this new family experience would not be forgotten. Mom would work hard to ensure this event of roll passing would not happen again—that is when she started baking bread and not serving rolls.

Dad, however, found a way to get back in the game. He loved to eat out and would order rolls. The tradition continued. There was nothing Mom could do about it.

Today, the tradition continues. It has been passed on to our children and grandchildren. Now it is bad manners to not pass the rolls.

Sometimes the simplest gesture of something as trivial as launching a roll to the person who requested it brings forth a practice that becomes an affirmative memory for a family group.

Patton Court dinners held the heartfelt expression of laughter, the commitment of love, and the opportunity to dine with people who believed in many of the same values, family.

CHAPTER EIGHT

SITTING ON SINGING PINES PORCH

Let your conversation always be full of grace, seasoned with salt, so that you may know how to answer everyone.

—Colossians 4:6

Mom and dad outside Singing Pines cabin. Note the large porch where conversations were served here many nights of the summer.

Our summer home had a porch that extended about the width of the structure. As a family, we seldom sat there to watch the world go by. Not that the porch was uncomfortable; the wicker rockers were there for just that, rest and comfort. They did what a rocking chair could do.

Occasionally, Dad would elect to take a few moments and go out and sit, rock, smoke, or chew on his cigar. This opportunity to have a family porch sit-down happened only a few times a summer. Mom would recognize the opportunity and would get lemonade or coffee ready. I would find a railing to sit on and perch myself there. Better to watch the unfolding story, which I knew would happen.

Because there was a road running to other staff housing at the front of the porch, people would stop by to talk. I suspect Dad's objective was just that, an informal staff meeting.

Dad would wait, watching the ebb and flow of traffic, the staff and guests walking by. Sometimes you could hear the music from square dancing in one of the meeting rooms in the line of sight from our porch.

The summer sun would be setting, and you could watch the creep of evening shadows ascend the mountain named Teddy's Teeth, after President Teddy Roosevelt, and like a summer blanket being pulled up for a night's sleep, the final shadow of the day progressed until there was a promise of morning with the settling of dusk capturing the end of the day.

Our time for family was generally cut short, in my opinion, because summer or full-time staff would see Dad sitting, which in itself was unusual, and would seize the opportunity to talk to him about a maze of subjects.

They would come and sit in one of the rockers, and the conversation would start about weather, lodging being almost full, or any of the myriad of subjects concerning the operation of the Y camp.

It was a staff meeting, informal like all the others, but a time to hash out challenges. Dad always said there were no problems, only opportunities, and the group sitting there would look for ways to solve "opportunities" so that guests would have the optimal vacation experience possible.

Mom would bring out refreshments, the lemonade and coffee, cookies all on a plate designed to help nourish the discussion at hand.

Occasionally a cabin donor would drop by and become part of the group meeting. Many deals were accomplished on our corporate family porch, from making sure there was enough good food available for the coming conference to a family agreeing to donate a cabin. It just happened in the comfort of a mountain summer evening high in the Rockies, rocking in a wicker chair, refreshments included.

Because there was little television in the fifties, entertainment came in the form of just getting together. I see the front porch times being lost in today's current active society.

Some would say when you sit on the front porch, you watch the world go by. I believe you are setting many times the direction the world will be traveling by the conversations you have. When you are watching from a child's vantage point, you see things in a different perspective. The staff would just come and sit and talk about Y things, operations going on, etc. But the caveat of discussion would come when educators, successful businessmen, national coaches, and athletes would climb the five steps to the porch and sit and chat.

Dreams were formed, discussed, and implemented. "What you need is a building of Texas steel," stated Henry Dorsey, cabin donor, businessman, and friend of Dad. He was referring to a rather large youth group that was scheduled to hold a national conference one year out. Dad had rented a circus tent for the gathering, but that was not good enough for a citizen of the Lone Star state. Texas steel was needed for a meeting place. As the conversation continued, not only a meeting place but dorms under the meeting room, storage, and a bowling alley would be added. The building dream kept getting bigger and bigger, and Dad just listened and gave gentle nudges of direction.

Over the next hour, a place, a purpose, and a mental design was launched. I am sure there were more meetings about structure, costs, and all the usual construction issues of a new building. What I found out later was, not much was discussed with the YMCA of the Rockies board of directors. They would soon be aware of the construction by seeing the gaping hole in the ground where the aptly named Long House was being built for the next summer.

Henry wanted to build the structure, and he had the construction connections and a summer to do just that.

CHAPTER NINE

FIVE CENTS FOR BOB

For if the willingness is there, the gift is acceptable according to what one has.

—2 Corinthians 8:12

There was a time when grocery stores were a gathering place for not only sustenance but conversation as well. At one time there was a fairly well stocked grocery store on the grounds where Y guests and staff could pick up supplies they forgot or didn't have. There was just about everything you needed to complete your food needs based on your vacation.

The grocery store was operated by a retired individual with a background as a grocer. I guess retirement does not come easily to the supplier of food and dry goods.

We would purchase most of our summer needs at the store. Because our meals were supplied, most of what we needed were breakfast items, eggs, bacon, cereal, and such. Mom would make up a list of needed items, and it was my duty to go to the grocery and get the items and bring them back home. This securing of food was a weekly ritual that was requested and performed as a family obligation as any child would do.

The walk to the grocery store was not far and was downhill, which meant the walk home with the nutritional treasurers was uphill, the reverse would have been preferred because of the bags of groceries that needed to be toted home.

"Here is the list, I added five cents for you," Mom would always say. That was the treat and reward for the labor used. I would start my trek to the store with a mental list of what the five cents would purchase for me. Candy, cookies, gum, chips, so much to choose from. There was no direct path a person would take, but one path was logs placed together to form ground barriers for cars not to cross. The logs were laid on the ground with short length logs running perpendicular to keep them together, which meant you had the opportunity to walk on them and let your imagination explode with possibilities as to where you were and what you were walking across.

I would consider many scenarios for the always-dangerous and death-defying expanse. Sometimes the log walk would be over a rushing cavernous river filled with killer piranha. Of course the river was in a dangerous foreign country. It would be a matter of life and death to cross. Only a person with the supreme skill of balance, daring, and a chance for danger would and could make the torturous passage. Other times, a steel high beam of a skyscraper would be the adventure in terror. Each undertaking in my mind was a challenge to succeed. The log expanse was around one hundred yards long, so the walk to stay on and balanced was a lengthy challenge.

Over time, of a few minutes, the level of walking on the horizontal logs became less and less a challenge, until I lost my balance, which happened often. As your equilibrium was starting to go, your arms flailed to maintain your dominance over the log and not be cast into the depths of whatever fantasy you were a part of in your mind's eye. Then you stumbled off the log and landed on the reality of the ground. That of course didn't stop you because miraculously you survived the plunge and continued your journey.

Finally, after a dangerous journey, you arrived at the grocery store, list intact and ready for the next now-mundane mission in life, picking up what was ordered.

"Hi, Mr. Phillips. Mom sent me with a list of things we needed."

"I know, she called and said you were on your way. Let me see the list and we will get things going."

She called, I thought. We are not even looking at a mile from the house. What could possibly happen in that distance? Mothers are beyond overprotective. All I did was cross a cavern of piranha, man-eating fish, almost fall in the raging waters but escaped death because of well-honed survival skills. Mom called ahead—embarrassing, to say the least.

The list would be gathered and placed in two to three paper grocery sacks, of which I was assigned to carry—uphill—to our home.

"Can you sign the charge ticket?" Mr. Phillips would ask. Could I sign? I may be a kid, but I am a world adventurer kid. Of course I could sign the charge ticket. Didn't I defy eternal rest just getting here?

"The list says there is five cents for you. What would you like?" This is where the kid returns and the brave explorer exits.

There is so much to choose from, but the choice is always the same. I would select an ice cream bar covered with chocolate. There has never been any other choice. Even today a vanilla ice cream bar coated with chocolate is an anytime treat.

That selection required waiting a few minutes to consume the treasure, but of course, the path back would also have its set of challenges to conquer carrying three bags of groceries in paper sacks that could burst apart for no reason except to get me in trouble.

Having the proper nourishment was vital to the brave traveler bringing much-needed supplies back to his parents, and it was time to set off.

"Bye, Mr. Phillips. Thanks for helping me get the groceries."

"No problem, Bobby, see you in a few days," he said as he picked up the phone. I knew he was calling my mother, saying I was on my way back.

Wasn't I an explorer willing to risk life and limb to secure needed supplies for survival? Well, at least groceries.

As I trekked up the ever-increasing hill to our house and the challenge of summiting a steep mountain came into focus, once again I would have to cross a large ice glacier, balancing the sacks for food to get to the other side and to safety. There was, only a log to cross, but the log had snow on it and ice. This would require all the skill of an athlete and the bravery of a valiant explorer to succeed. I had it covered. After all, even with breakable items in the sack, this crossing was nothing to worry about.

I placed one foot in front of another, walking across the dangerous passing. Each step contained confidence and a bit of pride. The further I traveled across the treacherous crossing, the more exhilarated I felt. I was the best, the bravest, and the most daring. Then it happened; again losing my delicate balance was far easier toting bags of food than before when I could use my arms for regaining my balance. I used my arms just as before and immediately realized my fatal error. The bags of groceries went flying as I fell from the log and from grace.

I had forgotten about the eggs and the milk in a glass container. In an instant a dozen eggs became scrambled and mixed with milk, cereal, and other food items not edible ever again.

The explorer in me was gone and the possible future of me becoming an adult could be in question. Three bags of reality lay on the ground, and I needed to come up with a good reason for the carnage I had caused.

Disappeared was the thrill of being an explorer, and present was the child desperately coming up with a reasonable cause to cover the cost of destruction. I could not even come up with a good excuse or reason to offer. I picked up what I could of what was left, placed them in the torn bags, and took the smallest steps possible home, delaying the inevitable.

Mom met me at the door with a "What happened?" look. Perhaps there was hope for a less-than-reasonable story to tell her; I considered that for less than a moment. "I fell," was all I could come up with at the time. The brave explorer really had no good excuse or brave story to convey. The explorer had departed, and so was the prowess of a brave individual seeking out adventure; present was just a kid with sacks of broken food and a broken fantasy. Reality set in like concrete being poured; each moment the reality became more solid.

What I thought would be an ending became a beginning of understanding grace, trust, and love of a parent. "Are you OK?" Mom asked. "What happened?"

"I was trying to walk on the logs and I lost my balance, and I fell." That was all my now tearstained face and voice could offer. "I am sorry." Final answer.

Mom was assured I was not hurt. She took what was left of the groceries, placed them on the counter, and did an inventory. I stood there, waiting for the next whatever to fall; I knew it would. Then she took pencil and paper in hand and started writing something.

"Here is what I want you to go and get," she said as she handed me a new grocery list. "Go back to the store and bring home what was broken."

I did this task willingly. What I learned was far more valuable than just replacing what was broken.

What was mended was a lesson in forgiveness and understanding. Grace was extended by offering understanding and forgiveness. Love was displayed in the process of knowing kids are simply kids, and there are times dreams and adventures of the mind get mixed with the gravity of reality.

There is a lot to be learned by a simple grocery list, more than the gathering of groceries. The chance of honesty in a child, the showing of love from a parent, and the reward of a second chance far outweighed the gift of five cents for Bob. However, the ice cream always did taste wonderful on a warm summer day.

CHAPTER TEN

FOURTH OF JULY AT THE YMCA OF THE ROCKIES

Now the Lord is the Spirit, and where the Spirit of the Lord is, there is freedom.

—2 Corinthians 3:17

The fourth of July is our nation's Day of Independence, but according to England's history books, the event is called Insurrection Day. Whatever you title the day, at the Y camp this was a day of a carnival feeling, an event for a parade, and the opportunity to appreciate the sacrifices made to harbor the freedoms of the United States.

The Fourth of July was the emotional and unofficial halfway point of the summer experience for the college staff and was the opportunity to celebrate the birth of our nation with guests and staff. This opportunity was not overlooked in anyway. Many families and guests would purposely plan their vacation around the YMCA Fourth of July celebration. Every year this was an event not to be missed.

There was the parade with each department competing for "best of" to secure bragging rights for the duration of the summer. The parade carried a theme each year that would reflect what the Fourth of July stood for. Work, for the most part, came to a standstill on the Fourth as staff lined up for the parade with their departments' float midmorning.

The planning and fun started with secret preparation well before parade day. Housekeeping, Maintenance, Youth Program, Kitchen, Office, and Livery would meet independently to decide on a type of celebration display to design and construct in hopes of securing the coveted Best of Theme award. The floats would have to be constructed the night of July 3. Secrecy was important, and building and decorating the department float needed to be done clandestinely, sometimes just before sunrise as to have the surprise advantage of being awarded that coveted honor of being the "best of" for that year.

Perhaps the caveat of the day came from the day care and the youth program. Counselors would have to prepare the children in costume and get the kids ready on short notice that morning of the Fourth. This was close to herding cats on catnip or nailing Jell-O to a tree in a stiff breeze. Persistent, the counselors were to achieve the task at hand.

The fourth of July parade was always a summer highlight for summer staff and guests. The tradition of celebrating this is part of the DNA of the YMCA of the Rockies.

The Administration Building was decorated for many years with red, white, and blue buntings. Extra flags were displayed, and patriotic music was played before, during, and after the parade. Housekeeping choir many times sang the national anthem as the flag was raised. The main road in front of the Ad Building was the parade route from Jellison Infirmary to Hyde Chapel. And dining room chairs and folding chairs lined the walkway for guests and staff to have a place to sit and watch. However, most people were caught up in the moment and stood. The parade was named "the biggest little parade in the USA" by Chaplain Bill Huth in the 1980s. To say families and people came from across the nation to witness the largest little Fourth of July parade would be an accurate statement.

There was a master of ceremonies chosen, and different each year, describing every float. A group of three to five judges was selected from the staff and guests to rate and award trophies in several different categories to the departments. It was a small vacation resort with a big heart that hosted an over-the-top celebration of independence and freedom.

Every year the creativity of summer staff never ceased to amaze me and the crowd blessed with being a part of a two-hundred-plus-year independence celebration. Somehow water hoses and buckets of candy were an annual thing. Maintenance staff would be on the lookout for their department head so they could "bless" him with a soaking from the fire engine water hose. They were never a good aim, and collateral damage was large. The morning was warm, and the cold water was a surprise welcome.

Bribery could be witnessed as some departments had taken up a collection for the tossing of candy to the spectators and special gifts for the judges. The candy worked for the children watching the parade, but candy never worked for the judges; however, homemade cookies and cakes were never turned down by the selected judge committee, or shared for that matter.

Tributes in the displays were focused on those who gave their lives so this day could be celebrated. When the national anthem was sung and the Pledge of Allegiance was spoken, there was a reverence in remembrance and thankfulness for the sacrifice and what the USA stood for in the world. The Y chaplain give an invocation as all stood heads bowed, thanking the Lord for the guardianship of the precious freedom bestowed on the nation and its citizens.

The parade was small-town celebration in a resort setting at high altitude. People's lives would be impacted by the recognition of the freedom precious to the citizens of the United States of America. College students from foreign countries learned of the flavor of freedom and gained a greater educational and emotional understanding of the precious gift of freedom, independence, and opportunities within the borders of the USA.

The American flag was carried at the beginning of the parade by the wranglers at the livery, an honor never given up to another department; along with the American flag were the Colorado and Christian flags displayed at the parade center. The national anthem was played as the American flag was raised; the department head of maintenance was given this honor. If a new flag was needed because Old Glory was torn and tattered from the sun, wind, and elements, this was the time to retire one and place in service the other.

From the Ad Building porch, a person could watch the raising of the flag of freedom and look across at the mountains with Mount Ypsilon rising 13,520 feet into the Colorado sky, emphasizing even more the choice of freedom paid for by many so many more could embrace this precious gift.

The kitchen crew—not to be outdone—had the task of creating a float and then rushing back to the process of fixing a typical Fourth of July lunch. This meal was at one time open to all who would like to have lunch. Hot dogs, hamburgers, potato salad, watermelons were always available for the hungry citizens. It was an all-you-can-eat freedom event served with a love of giving back something for everything America represented.

At one time the summer staff hosted an evening carnival in the center court of what was staff housing, known as the Mummy Quad. There were booths of many challenges of skill and prizes a young child really wanted but did not need. Each booth required a ticket or two, and those were purchased and all proceeds given to a chosen charity in the area. The kitchen crew garnered the greatest proceeds of dollars. They had an edge, a cake walk, cookie and dessert sale. Maintenance maintained order with a weakly constructed jail. One could place a warrant out for someone (cost involved depending on organizational standing) and place them in jail. The jail was construed out of bed springs latched together. The challenge was to break out or be "legally" released because your fine was paid by another. You were not allowed to buy your way out. Small people had an advantage on being able to break out, but they had a disadvantage as they could not run as fast the adult deputy who would find that person and would oftentimes be re-incarcerated. The previous escape route was fixed; this was always a work in progress. Eventually a benevolent deputy of the sheriff maintenance department would have pity on that person and release one back into the freedom of the celebration. The reasoning was that the carnival could not generate income if everyone was in the slammer.

The evening of July 4ᵗʰ was the annual carnival. Each department was responsible for some sort of a booth. The jail was reserved for maintenance the object was not to get in jail but if you were jailed, then the goal was to escape!

If the emotional high came from the parade, the sugar high was from the carnival and the treats that lasted for several hours into the evening. The day after the Fourth of July was back to serving guests and recalling the memories of the previous day.

As the parade ended and the carnival closed, the floats that were displayed in front of the Ad Building for those to admire for a few hours were dismantled and the vehicles placed back in service. Lunch was over, and staff were back to work, doing what they did best, serving the guests who had traveled to the Colorado Rockies.

Old Glory waved in the breeze, the parade chairs had been picked up long ago, and vacationing as usual had resumed. The street where the celebration took place was back to transporting traffic. The day was done, but the memory of the day continued to be celebrated in the memories of all who were involved.

In many ways, this rural celebration of American freedom has been lost with the large events and entertainment factors generated on the Fourth of July. But what is important is not the celebration, not the events, but the chance to pause and remember the date the world became free in a new country flexing its eagle's wings and declaring that all men had equal and unalienable rights, including the right inscribed in the First Amendment, the five pillars of the Constitution, freedom of religion, speech, press, assembly, and petition.

That is what the celebration of the Fourth is about and the honoring of those who fought to guarantee those freedoms.

It was a day to remember.

CHAPTER ELEVEN

DAY CAMP IN THE MID-1950s

Start children off on the way they should go, and
even when they are old they will not turn from it.
—Proverbs 22:6

Back before Sweet Memorial, Jellison Youth Building, or Legett Youth Building were constructed, parents would sign up their children for youth program in the Ad Building. Because this process took a few minutes, us kids were shuffled out to the Ad Building steps, where I would come up with a plan for riches. That memory is next.

We would be placed sitting on the steps. Guests could maneuver around each side; however, we were the youthful, driving, game-playing, singing force on the steps looking over the vast field to the mountains in the distance.

Each day we would sing, sit, jump up, sit down all to singing songs that required this activity. As the other children registered and they would eventually join, the crowd of youth grew in size, along with the volume of song and laughter.

The counselors recognized we were full of energy from sleep and most likely a sugary breakfast. Keeping us in control was not an option, but it was a challenge as kids giggled, shoved, and wiggled en mass, trying to top the other behavior around them. I was a master of energy. I knew the routine better than any other child here. They were around for a week, maybe two; my time spent was ten or more weeks. I could get things moving, and I did.

We would play hand and jumping games, sing song after song, anything to shave some of the energy of sugar and excitement down or directed another way. The youth counselors were experts at keeping the crowd in a group and together. They were masters of an instant game, making up new ones as needed.

One of the songs we sang was "Kookaburra Sits in the Old Gum Tree." The words make little sense, but when singing them, perfect logic abounds of times in a camp, then add hand gestures and you have the makings of a Broadway production.

Kookaburra sits on the old gum tree,
Merry merry king of the bush is he.
Laugh, Kookaburra, laugh, Kookaburra,
Gay your life must be!
Kookaburra sits in the old gum tree
Eating all the gumdrops he can see
Stop, Kookaburra, Stop, Kookaburra
Leave some there for me.
Kookaburra sits in the old gum tree,
Counting all the monkeys he can see
Stop, Kookaburra, Stop, Kookaburra,
That's no monkey, that's me.

The group would sing and sing this tune over and over, finally moving on to classics such as "She Will Be Coming Around the Mountain," "The Itsy-Bitsy Spider"—the list went on. At some point the high-energy songs gave way to songs and lyrics directed toward God. "Jacob's Ladder" was generally the opening of a new singing direction, ending with "Kym Ba Ya."

Energy of the body had been redirected to focus on energy of the soul. We were quieter now. Reverence was taught, and this was a time of respect and honoring Christian values.

The day's group was complete, and only a few other opening tasks were needed. Staff was introduced as each day there were new faces that didn't know the names of the youth counselors. Rules were discussed and sack lunches gathered in appropriate age groups.

We all walked across Administration Avenue, the main thoroughfare in front of the Ad Building to the flagpole where we recited the Pledge of Allegiance with hands over your heart, and this pose was held as the flag was raised. It was an honor to be chosen to hold the folded American flag and to untie the flagpole rope that would hoist the flag of freedom to the heavens. You always hoped you were among the chosen few. Once the flag was hoisted to its proper height, a counselor would secure the rope; the reverse process would be repeated at the end of the day.

A prayer was offered by a senior counselor. This was a privilege awarded to second-year college staff and held in personal respect. We all bowed our heads. Some nervous giggles would break out before the "amen." That would be discussed later in the day.

Now divided up into appropriate age groups, we were off on a day adventure of exercise, exploring and knowing there was an opportunity to create a new friendship.

Personal projects at the Craft Room was a highlight as you were welcomed to decide on what you would like to create. It was the shortest walk; only a few yards and you were there. The longest walk was to the livery. We lined up like ducks, two by two wherever we would walk to. The stables, as they were called, were down a small hill. You had a great overlook of the horses as you approached, but you knew you were close if the wind was right. Generally, the horseback ride was about an hour on the trail. The view to the left and right was nature. The view ahead was the person and backside of the horse; you stayed in line. Only the wranglers could canter alongside, keeping their herd of charges in line and safe.

After an hour, the group gathered for the walk up what had been a small hill and now was a mountain accented by a sheer cliff. I never figured out how a small hill at the beginning of the ride could gain so much height when the ride was completed, but it did each time.

Lunch would be served in various places, and your sack lunch would appear like magic. Being kids, the nutrition needs were present every minute, but you had to wait until each person had their lunch. Prayer was offered, and at the "amen," sack lunches were torn open. Sandwiches were kept in wax bags; fruit, chilled in the morning, was day temperature now. Milk was always cold and was part of the day camp offering, as well as an afternoon snack. Lunchtime was a time to wonder about the rest of the day, which was generally kept secret.

We completed our lunch, and depending on your age, you went to another activity or were required to take a nap. Afternoons went fast, and soon it was time to gather once again on the steps of the Ad Building for final thoughts and good-byes for the day. Some kids you thought you would see the next day but you never saw them again; they were gone, traveling home early or another family activity. If you had something to say, best say it before you were picked up; it could be your only chance.

As parents rejoined the family, the youth counselors would give a brief report about the day and behavior of the day camp child. A lot of kids didn't see that coming.

I was just dismissed to find my way home or to some destination on the way home, which I generally opted for. I would look at magazines at the Bookstore, check out the candy inventory at the Rustic Room, talk to the Front Desk staff, or see if Dad was in his office—he generally wasn't. I would talk a few minutes to his secretary, Lucille Miller. Eventually, I would wander toward home and my boy cave. I was tired, but not too tired to stop by Maintenance and discover Dad talking to the staff. He was OK, and I was satisfied the world was turning properly.

Arriving home after a day of hard playing and exploring, Mom would have a snack ready for me, bribery to come home. Cookies and milk were the standard fare and was appreciated by a hungry growing kid.

We would talk about the day, hers and mine. I would grab a comic book or magazine and find my usual boy place to read, eventually walking up when called to go to the employee dining room for the evening meal.

The day was complete, and tomorrow would hold another unknown adventure with new and familiar kid faces. The same songs would be sung, the flag raised, we would recite the Pledge of Allegiance, and the day would progress.

Each day was a treasure to experience. Each day in part influenced your life in some way and impacted your thinking and life direction. You just didn't know or realize it at the time, but looking back, the pledge to the flag, the songs, the prayers opening and closing the day formed the mold of who I became.

All this was a gift from God, who knew ahead of time what the day would bring. The day was done, and so was I. Tomorrow would be another great day.

CHAPTER TWELVE

THE AD BUILDING, MONEY, AND MATCHES

The greedy stir up conflict, but those who trust in the Lord will prosper.

—*Proverbs 28:25*

The Administration Building was built in 1910 and almost burned down in the early 1950s, but not from lighting, or anything nature caused. The building was originally designed as the social and dining hall. Over time the focus of the Ad Building changed to a place for the administration of the YMCA of the Rockies to have a functional location to operate and for guests to check in, get a cup of coffee, write postcards, and many other activities. It was also a gathering place for staff, but mostly for guests.

At the entrance to the building and up from the massive stairway that connected the wraparound porch was the bookshop. One would walk up the stairs, where day camp would gather each morning, have an opening sing-along, and move on with daily activities. During this opening time of day camp, I noticed adults would go to the bookstore, purchase a paper or a magazine, and would be given some change and exit the way they came, mostly placing their change in their pocket. I reasoned some of the change must have fallen through the cracks between the boards on the stairs. I figured there would be a small fortune to be found under those stairs that I sat on during weekdays watching the purchase of products. All I needed to do was find a way to the fortune, and the riches would be mine, all mine.

Good plan, I thought, and well worth an adventure on an unsupervised Saturday. Or so that was what I thought, and as I assumed there was a fantastic fortune, the treasure of coins became bigger and bigger in my imagination.

Finally on a Saturday morning, it was time to place my money-retrieving plan into action. There was an access door that allowed a person to be under the building, but the door was at the opposite end of where the stairs were. It would be a long crawling trek to the front of the building from the back of the structure, but worth every penny, nickel, dime, and quarter that was there. Sounded reasonable to me.

The plan was to wait until the access was open, crawl through the dirt, find the stairs, wiggle my way under the descending stairs, retrieve the silver, reverse the process, and get out, no one will be the wiser. Simple, efficient, nothing to it except for dirty clothes and a pocketful of change, well worth the effort. It was a done deal in a child's mind. What could possibly go wrong? Nothing.

I would take a few matches just in case it was dark in my journey. That was the only supply provision I could see that I needed. Matches, desire, reward, daring—perfect plan.

On the specified Saturday, I was up early, ready and excited about my clandestine operation. Only I knew what I was about to do. After all, when retrieving a fortune, best to keep to yourself what you are doing.

As I arrived at the access door, there was a lock hanging from the hasp—challenge number one. I noticed it was fake locked. It looked like the door was secure, but the lock hung there, and all that was needed was to twist the padlock and you were in. I waited for the perfect time when there weren't adults entering or exiting the building. I pretended to be playing in the vicinity, ready to go to the next level of the adventure. Finally, there was a break, and I twisted the lock, pushed the door open, and shut the door, keeping the lock so as to secure my escape route safe. It was dark under the Ad Building, but I had matches. I brought more than I figured I needed. I had light.

My imagination was running wild as I thought I was the only person in years that had been under the building. The cavern of dirt, darkness, and overhead structure were freighting, but the goal of financial solvency spurred me forward. Forward across dirt with critter "evidence," and for the first time I realized I might not be the only living creature under here. I dismissed that thought as much as I could, reasoning I was bigger than them and I could defend myself. After all, I had fire; they didn't.

After crawling for what seemed hours but in reality was only a few minutes, I could see the dim light through the stairs. My goal was within reach, and my pockets were ready to be filled. Emotions ran high for this under-the-building adolescent explorer. It was time to reap the reward of observation and careful planning; a windfall was close at hand.

I still could not see well enough as there was dirt settling through the stairs as people above me walked up and down. I scrapped the loose dirt and discovered a few coins, but not what I had expected, yet the thought of more spurred me on. Perhaps if I was closer to where the stairs started, in that small space I knew, I would discover the massive coins I just knew were there. I moved further and further out in the creepy, crawly underground staircase. The more I moved forward, the darker it became for some reason.

But I had matches. I had light, and light was what I needed! That would be the solution to the discovery, light, and the coins would glitter like the lost treasure it was. I lit a match. Yes, there was a dime, and the match went out. I noticed there was a lot of scrap paper under the stairs and wondered how that got there, but I wasn't there for paper unless it was a dollar bill. That thought spurred on my drive to continue to light a match, look, and hopefully find something and build my financial empire. I seemed to be using a lot of matches and not finding as many coins as I thought, and not one dollar was to be had either.

I needed to go just a few feet further under the decreasing space in the stairs. That would be where the loot was, I reasoned. On my belly and reaching out in front of me, I struck a match, looked and looked and found nothing, nothing but a bunch of trash. Then I felt it, the burning of fire on my fingers. Instinctively I dropped the match, and the fire found paper. I had light, but I didn't need light now. There was no treasure, but there were flames, and I knew that was not good at all.

Because the space was confined, all I could do was beat the ever-increasing paper fire with my hand and using both hands to stop the flames from getting any bigger. After what seemed like a lifetime, the fire was out, and there was smoke to prove it. I knew the wood was old and dry, the building older than time itself, and I had just put out a fire! Was I a hero? Probably not, and I was not rich either. There were a few coins, not the amount I expected. My fingers hurt from the match that burned them, and the top of my hands were sore from hitting the stairs while I was beating out the fire. Adrenaline had taken over during that time. I was alive, the building was not going to burn down, and I was on my way back out.

As I crawled back to where I came in, I thought it odd that I had not heard as many footsteps at the end of suppressing the fire as I heard at the beginning of looking for money. Odd, but I dismissed that thought as I saw there was more light coming from the access door. Funny, I thought, I had closed the door, and now it was partially open. Must have opened on its own, I thought.

As I got closer to the door, the escape route, I noticed a pair of shoes that looked familiar. They were standing just outside. I could not place where I had seen them before, but I knew that I knew them somehow. About the time I stuck my head out the access door, I realized they were my dad's shoes. That was also when I was launched from the escape route to the reality it was my dad, and he was not pleased with me. I believed this might be my last hour on earth.

Being relatively small in stature and dad being an extremely large man and possessing an attitude to match his stature I just knew this adventure was over was not going to end well at all. "What are you doing?" was the question. I thought it best not to answer. "Answer me now." That was not a request but a directive that I better follow immediately. I was then placed back on mother earth; I had been suspended by my shirt and belt. Dad and I had been seeing eye to eye.

I didn't have a lot of time to craft a well-defined answer, and the intense glare of a parent spoke volumes about answering quickly, honestly, and hopefully with a response that would protect my backside from too much damage that I knew was coming.

The explanation I gave I cannot remember, but I do remember that, like Moses, I stuttered, stammered, and tried to explain that I should be let go. That was not the case and was not going to happen. Dad did listen, but the chiseled look of authority and parental oversight was not diminishing, and whatever I was going to say, did say, was not going to help.

"Follow me." Dad walked off, and I followed him around to the front of the Ad Building. The YMCA had an old fire truck that was reclaimed probably from World War II, and there it was standing guard at the stairway. Maintenance men were holding a small fire hose, looking at the stairs that were now wet, I wondered what they were doing and why they were washing the stairs, but only for a moment. They were there because someone had seen smoke and alerted someone else, which elicited a response from the fire truck, which I never saw running except on the Fourth of July.

Dad stood there. I was captured by his hand on my neck. "You could have created a real disaster." I thought I was going to be the destruction in process. The volunteer fire crew was cleaning up, people were getting back to normal, I was alive for the moment, and Dad was not happy. "I think you should go straight home. I will talk to you later." I knew what that could mean.

It was the longest day of my short life. Dad calmed down by dusk. I invested a lot of time in my room. Mom was expecting me as I arrived home, the miracle of phone calls from parent to parent.

The access door was now locked. I checked the lock occasionally. I was alive and not rich. Over the next few years I tried to analyze where the plan went wrong and came up with several decisions.

First of all, my imagination took over. Sinbad's fortune was not under the stairs, nor would it ever be. Number two, matches and paper are not your friends. Number three, imagination again was not a friend for the fortune seeker, except in books and movies; life doesn't happen that way. Number four, and perhaps the most understood in my youth, consider your exit route. The access door was within eyesight of Dad's office. The door was unlocked for no good reason.

The best-laid plans have unknown diversions, but life is full of lessons. I learned a valuable life direction lesson that day. Actions have consequences, and one, at any age, should think what that decision and action will result in. I didn't get a spanking, but all day in my room was punishment enough, wondering what was coming for punishment that I deserved.

A day's adventure turned into a day in my boy cave with nothing to do and no fortune. But I was richer in life because I realized life, my life, affects other lives. That lesson was worth more than any coins I found, which was less than fifty cents, of which I placed in the staff appreciation fund to be shared by all, a ransom well paid.

CHAPTER THIRTEEN

CHOOSING A CANDY BAR AT THE RUSTIC ROOM

Jesus answered, "If you want to be perfect, go, sell your possessions and give to the poor, and you will have treasure in heaven. Then come, follow me.
—Matthew 19:21

There are many defining events in a young boy's life. Selecting the right, proper candy bar is a mountaintop experience. There are certain standards and desires you need to recognize before you make the sweet selection.

First, there is chocolate, and will the selection be short lasting, long lasting (how a candy bar can be long lasting is beyond me at any age)? With or without nuts, melt in your mouth, in your hand—many choices. You approach the incredible variety that is available and just looking at what you must choose from; it takes a young boy's breath away. From Hershey's to Mars products, Nerds, to wrapped cheese crackers (forget those) and all kinds of sweet products, every one of which guaranteed to give you a sugar high, which was not recognized in the mid-1950s.

With excitement, fear, and anticipation I would walk up to the candy counter and start counting all the selections to choose from. I didn't care if I held up other customers. All I wanted was the opportunity to select the perfect sweet treat. This selection process was important to a sugar junkie, and chocolate was always at the top of the list.

Freda Teague was the manager of the Rustic Room and could be listed as one of the most patient persons in the world. She never rushed me and would make suggestions for a selection, and all that came with a Kansas kind of attitude of servant focus every summer she was present. Mid-May to just after Labor Day, there she was sitting by the cash register, helping customers, staff, and in all that, training new college staff each summer the value of serving while working.

Freda Teague (back row 5th from center) was the Rustic Room manager for many years. You could always find a staff meeting with management conducted in the afternoon around 3:00 most every day of the week at the back of the Rustic Room. The candy bar counter was located at the entrance to the Rustic Room, next to the popcorn machine.

Perhaps in her quiet, easy farming value way, this commitment to working with college staff was her gift to their future. If there ever was a candy salesperson slash psychologist, that would be Freda. "Bobby, I don't think you have ever tired this one," she would say, and I would consider that selection, but I was and still am a chocolate kind of guy. Going for something other than a cocoa bean product was a stretch of the sugar pallet.

We would talk through the selection process and mix that part of life with other topics. "How is your Mom doing? Did you go to the movie the other night? What did you think of it?" Freda would always turn the conversation away from the primary selection process to questions that would inevitably lead to a thought process of life's values. "I noticed in the movie that the main character had to lie to get out of trouble. Do you think that is right?"

All I wanted was to select the perfect candy bar, not to discuss the value of truth verses lies, but there I was stuck without a decision, and now I had to think about my answer on truth and lies. Life is never simple for a small sugar-needing boy with candy money to burn.

I knew I could not pay for what I wanted until we had our life discussion on lies and truth. It would be useless to try to redirect the conversation.

"I guess it depends on the reason for the lie," I stated, knowing this answer would not be acceptable. "So you think it is OK to lie in certain circumstances? Is that what you do?" Now we were into it, and the candy selection was moving further and further into the future.

"Well, no, maybe, it might be OK, but not really," I replied. "So where the Bible says 'do not lie' is not all correct?" Dang, I thought, could I have decided on a candy bar at another time when Freda, the truth seeker, was not here; then I realized she was always here, and I was stuck with my situation and dialogue until this verbal topic was completed.

"I don't know, could I have the chocolate bar with nuts, please," I requested. "When you answer the question, then you may," was Freda's reply.

What was this woman, I thought, the candy police, of justice, truth, and the American way?

Things with sugar were far, far away. I was considering starting Lent in the middle of the summer and not eating candy bars, and that was a bad idea. "I don't think anyone should lie, the truth is the best." That ought to settle it, and I will be on my way, sugar and all.

"Why do you think that now when just a few minutes ago you said, 'Lying might be OK, but not really.' What made you change your position so quickly?" The sugar high was beaming a sugar drought and a sugar low faster and faster. I could feel the money in my pocket, and I was starting to believe it would never leave the sanctuary where it was being held.

"Bobby, tell me this, if I said you can have this candy bar for free if you would tell a lie, would you accept the candy and lie to the person I told you to lie to?" For a second I thought we were making progress, then just like that the treat was snatched from my grasp.

Would I lie, deceive, falsify a statement for a candy bar? Lie, receive a candy bar; don't lie, kiss the free candy bar good-bye. I thought about that for only a moment.

"No, I don't think so, that would be wrong." Freda looked at me for a long time, it seemed like eternity. "You are right, lying is wrong, it is against one of God's specific commandments. Lying, deceit makes you lesser, not greater, and sorrows our God."

Good, we were making progress, and candy was closer . . . maybe.

"Honesty is a virtue that continually needs to be sought over and over every day. If you are not honest with a small thing, can you be trusted with anything?" Well, that was a thought to ponder for this young boy's sugar-starved soul.

"Many people lie all the time and don't realize it, but eventually they will be caught in their deception. Honesty is the best policy. There may be a time when you will be in trouble for telling the truth about something, but that trouble will be far less than the trouble you would have by lying and being found out later."

I soaked in Freda's words like the warmth of the sun. The main character in the movie lied, and it was portrayed as right, but it was wrong. I was caught in a deceptive teaching in a movie, and I started to think the deception was right when, in fact, it was wrong.

How many other values could be compromised that were wrong but seemed so right at the time? That was a lot for a young boy's mind to take in. I looked at Freda almost for the first time in the candy selection process. I saw a lady of incredible age, epic wisdom, and unconditional love looking back at me with the eyes of a teacher who realized the light had turned on and would continue to be light for my life.

Freda, Rustic Room manager, teacher of truth, caregiver to the sugar hungry. I never was told, nor did I ask what Freda did for a living, but what I did know was what she did for the living, the most important job. She cared, and she was willing to be involved on a personal scale in a young boy's life. She was committed to bringing value to a simple candy bar purchase.

I was thankful for the teaching and talks Freda and I had. I knew we would have many more times to talk and share because there was a lot of candy to decide on at the Rustic Room.

Freda was Freda, and I suspect I was one of the many students she taught lessons to. I know this because over time I heard from returning summer staff as they talked about working with this lady of the Rustic Room and she always touched the lives of whomever she talked to.

"I will take that candy bar," I said, "the one without nuts." It was smaller than most and would be easier to chew on. Freda handed it to me, and I gave her the required amount of change. However, the change I received was not in coin, but in recognizing, embracing, and understanding a value of life that would bode well every living day; that was the sweetest thing of the day.

CHAPTER FOURTEEN

DAD'S WINTER ACCIDENT

*You are my hiding place; you will protect me from
trouble and surround me with songs of deliverance.*
                                        —Psalm 32:7

*This photo was taken possibly the summer before the auto accident where dad
lost partial use of his hands. Look at the car in the background, although
grainy, you can see the type of metal bumper that was part of the design.
Author's photo*

I n the winter months of the early 1950s the Y camp was basically shut down except for a skeleton crew of grounds and maintenance staff, but that didn't stop Dad from traveling once or twice a week to Estes Park from Denver to see what needed to be done—or what was completed. I suspect also just to be with a winter staff at the end of a road in an area that was very much shut for the winter months.

Estes Park started its winter hibernation about noon on Labor Day and didn't wake up until just around Memorial Day in May. Even the one and only stoplight on the corner of Moraine and Elkhorn Avenue was covered with a burlap sack for the windy winter months.

Burlap Covering over a four-way stop light for the winter, who would have thought! Yet, for many winters, this was policy in Estes Park. Notice the snow in the center of the street. *Courtesy of the Estes Park Museum, 2006013381*

It was often joked but close to the truth that at two o'clock in the afternoon of Labor Day one could shoot a cannon down Moraine Avenue, and the cannon shot may be reported around Thanksgiving, investigated somewhere between Christmas and New Year, and forgotten about by Easter. Estes Park was as close to the definition of a ghost town in the winter except for a few necessary businesses, the local grocery store, Brodie's, and the government employees that worked for the town, and federal government; even those numbers were few.

That was part of the reasoning of Dad traveling to the Y camp. It was a lonely place and generally windy place with one snowy TV station from Cheyenne WY and a phone line was about it for any social or human interaction. At that time, Estes Park, in the winter, was at the end of the road.

There were exceptions for every schedule, and one Saturday Dad asked me if I would like to go to Estes with him. I could see a kid my own age, and we could hang out together for a few hours. Deal done, in the car, and we were off.

Denver wasn't snowing when we left Mom at home. She opted out to let the boys have a day. Being with Dad alone for the trip up and back amounted to a treasure trove of hours of companionship. Not that we talked a lot, we were just there, same car; it was windshield time accented by parent-child time.

The car was in good repair, new snow tires with walnut shells in the tread for traction. As we journeyed closer to Estes, the snow became heavier and thicker as we gained altitude. From Denver to Lyons (another hibernation town) was passable, but the real climb to Estes was starting at the town limits of Lyons.

Soon the road turned from dry pavement, to damp, to occasionally some snow to all snow and slick. I had confidence in my father's driving abilities. We all had been in snow conditions before and would be again and again. Yet the road and the snow seemed different this time, different like it was angry and mechanical things were not welcome in this weather. A few cars had slid off the road, and they signaled us to keep moving, because stopping would be just that, stopped. Colorado's snow plowing in the fifties was sufficient but not like the technology in the present day. When snow was on the road, the sun would eventually burn it off, and there was not any sunshine.

As we continued up the mountain road of curves, guardrails, there were places of an absence of guardrails where there were deep drop offs and threatening weather continued to push back the safety margin. "What do you think, should we turn back?" was the question Dad asked as we continued to slide and skid on the road. I wanted to see my friend, "No, it is OK, we should go on," I reasoned. Besides we were more than halfway there, on the side of a slippery sloped mountain, sliding on the road, and there really was not a place to stop, turn around, and head down. Also, that was defeat; we didn't set out to accomplish what we planned.

Dad was silent as we traveled further and further to Estes, the winter ghost town, and to camp. As we rounded the corner, we continued to lose more speed and momentum; there was a car blocking the road, and we needed to slow down to a crawl to get past the vehicle, which resulted in stopping and spinning warm tires on a cold, icy, snow-covered road. We were now stuck.

"Stay here, don't get out," Dad said. He didn't have to tell me twice. I was safe, warm, and not concerned. Not until the car started drifting backward and toward the cliff drop; that got my attention as Dad was not in the driver's seat.

The car slid slowly backward, and I could hear, but not see, people yelling and then screaming. After a few seconds, the vehicle came to an abrupt halt; it had hit something. I decided now there was action needed on my part. I scrambled out of the car on the driver's side as mostly what I could see was air on my passenger side, and I knew what that could mean.

As soon as my feet touched the snow-packed slick road, I took no less than a few steps and found myself inspecting the surface of the snow. The reality of how slick and dangerous the road had become came clearly into focus. It was really slick, and we didn't need to be here. Something was happening on the other side of the car, and I scooted and slid around there to discover Dad's hands bloodied and not looking anywhere near normal. "Give me your bandanna," a man said. It was not a request; it was a command. He wrapped one of Dad's hands and then wrapped the other hand. Dad looked like he was ready to box the way his hands were wrapped, and my red bandanna matched the other one that had been white and was turning redder as I watched.

I was instructed to get in the car, and a gentleman told Dad he would drive him to the doctor's office or hospital. That was when I knew we were in trouble, but I didn't know why.

"Your dad just saved your life," the gentleman told me. "If it wasn't for him grabbing the back bumper and pushing the car back on the road, you would have been a goner." I was told later the car was skidding between to wooden posts designed to show where the road ended and the cliff began, and Dad had seen the car move, got behind the car and gravity. He stopped the car by grabbing underneath the back bumper and pushing the car forward to a stop. The result was my life being spared and his tendons in his fingers not being spared; they were severed, and that is why his hands looked like they did and didn't work.

We traveled down the mountain with Dad using his forearms to steer the not-damaged car to a hospital in Longmont. Mom was still at home, not knowing anything about what had happened.

As we entered the emergency door of the hospital, there was a flurry of action of nurse whites and doctor coats. Dad was laid down on a rolling gurney and wheeled off to where I didn't know. All I did know was he was not coming back. Bravery lost to childhood at that instant, and the tears, choking breaths, and abject sense of loss took over. Never, never again was I going to see my father, and I really didn't thank him for saving my life, and besides, I was the one who said to press on. This was all my fault. The emotions of a scared, lonely child in an antiseptic-smelling room was just too much to handle. Besides the ride to the hospital had taken longer than dad had thought as he needed to stop more frequently to find more towels, rags, anything to keep the bleeding on his hands somewhat at bay.

Time stopped for this child, and there was no way I could see to wind the clock. Finally, after what seemed like an eternity, Dad came out with his hands bandaged in white. He looked older than I had ever seen him. "Time to go home, son." We did, and the drive was one of anticipation, concern, and an abiding love for my father. The roads were clear and dry, and that was good as Dad still had difficulty steering the car. We just went slower than I had ever seen Dad drive.

Arriving at our Denver home, I was told to go inside. I saw Dad back out. He had also told me to tell Mom he was on his way to the hospital closest to our home for surgery. I greeted Mom, and she mentioned we were home early and asked where Dad was. "He is on his way to the hospital for an operation." That statement stopped Mom in her tracks, and I explained as much as I could what had happened.

I had not been left alone in the house much before this time, but I was going to be now as Mom was out the door, in her car, and off to the hospital. I had not seen her move that fast ever.

Being alone isn't what you think it is when you are young and have never really been the only one in your house that way. Time dragged, and darkness settled in. I thought I was going to lose one parent and now two. Creepy darkness crawled in like black ink in a bottle, and I didn't want to turn on a lot of lights. I didn't know what to expect.

The doorbell rang, which startled me. Mom had called a neighbor to come over. I had an adult to keep the creepy darkness away and help still a child's fears. She explained what was going on and that Dad would not be home for a day or two and Mom would be here later that night. Dad was going to be OK, and Mom was coming home, world aligned and starting to feel safe.

Over the next year Dad would squeeze a rubber ball to strengthen what was left of the flexibility in his hands. Eight out of ten tendons had been severed and had to be reattached. I heard the doctor say he would never have the full use of his hands again. That didn't happen. He continued to do his therapy, never refusing to give up, never taking "never" for an answer, and not once complaining about pain, loss of dexterity, or the reason it happened.

Eventually, I forgave myself and for the incident. Dad told me one night as he was squeezing the handball, "It wasn't your fault, I could have turned around anytime. I wanted to go to camp too." Forgiveness, understanding, grace, and love, ingredients that mix well in a family recipe.

Dad never recovered complete use of his hands, but enough to live well and accept the challenge of not being able to make a fist or close your hand around an object. His physical grip was impaired, but that didn't stop him or even really slowed him down, just a fact of life, and I believe he saw it as a small payment to saving his young son's life.

For many years, my family has continued to travel the same road to Estes Park in clear and inclement conditions. As we would depart out the city of Lyons, my thoughts would go back to that snowy Saturday that I grew up faster than anticipated because of weather and a goal to achieve and a schedule to keep. God had other plans, plans to knit our family closer by avoiding a tragedy that could not have been repaired.

As I drive past the double curve in the road, I think of that day. There is a continual guardrail there now. Colorado has a better, safer system of plowing the roads. Years ago, on New Year's Eve, Barb, my wife, and I were moving to Estes Park from Evergreen, Colorado. It had been snowing, and we were driving in the inky dark. As we exited Lyons, a snowplow started to plow the road in front of us, and stayed ahead of our caravan all the way to the final descent into Estes Park.

With his flashing yellow and blue lights, a newly cleaned road, Barb in our small car, and me in the largest moving truck we could have rented, I thought back to that fateful Saturday when all of our world's changed, and now again the world is changing for us.

We passed the double curves safely. Time continued to advance, and we were in beat with where God wanted us. Some things change; others, the important ones, don't.

CHAPTER FIFTEEN

CHRISTMAS IN JULY

When the angels had left them, and gone into heaven, the shepherds said to one another, "Let's go to Bethlehem and see this thing that has happened, which the Lord has told us about."

—Luke 2:15

S inger Andy Williams recorded a popular song, "The Most Wonderful Time of the Year," referring to Christmas. At some point, Christmas in July was initiated on the twenty-fifth of the month at the Y. Christmas in July was originally intended just for summer staff as they would not be together for the season, so a celebration midsummer was a good idea to bring a staff family together.

A Christmas tree was selected, placed in the staff rec hall, and decorated with popcorn strings and paper chains. Strips of tin foil were cut for silver icicles, and a year-round staff family would offer to place into service a set of Christmas tree lights. Most decorations were created that summer. Only a few survived year to year. That was part of the beauty of this summer seasonal activity. The creating of Christmas in July is part of the memory magic that happens each year.

The anticipated activity of opening presents was reserved for a traditional Christmas Eve gathering. Homemade eggnog, punch, and Christmas cookies were set out in anticipation of a large staff/

family party. Presents were gathered for a week and placed under the tree. Because Christmas in July marked the middle of the summer, couple relationships between summer staff became elevated in many ways. Some would start to realize a commitment that would reach beyond just summer employment.

The rec hall was adorned in pine and spruce garland, and each year it seemed that more and more elaborate decorations appeared. The time became festive in celebration, not negating the birth of Christ.

Helen and Garland Matthews were staff counselors for many years, and Garland was the consistent yearly reader of the Christmas story. Remembering back, this is where the ugly sweaters may have started as this couple always, in midsummer's heat, had Christmas sweaters they wore that evening.

The eve of the Christmas party was an emotional anticipation because somewhere Santa would appear. Where the Santa costume was secured from is a lost secret and who was given the honor of this part changed each year. Some summers there was a Mrs. Clause; other summers, his children would too be part of the celebration. Still Santa would be rotund one summer, thin the next, sometimes a Southern accent, other times no accent. I never knew what Santa would appear; I just knew some form of a Santa representation would be present.

Before Santa would arrive to bring his seasonal joy, the singing of Christmas hymns was always a tradition. Employees would call out titles, and often a gifted pianist would play the close-to-in-tune piano; there was someone with a guitar and ukulele. There were years that the musical talent was more than abundant; gifted staff would sing a solo or play a hymn on their instrument of choice.

There was a year that the level of musical talent was epically high. For some reason a group was formed consisting of a violin, cello, and a makeshift bass. They played during part of the evening. It was a moment in timeless giving that no other three staff members could have done. Garland read, once again, the Christmas story as these three played. It was more than a Tiny Tim moment that was captured in time, but only for this moment. The lights turned low, the Christmas tree glittering, staff sitting around on the concrete floor. At the opposite end of the room a fire was crackling in the fireplace. Senior staff always were given any chair or couch that was available.

That year, I was standing looking at a room full of employees from many of parts of the United States. Some knew of Christmas with snow on the ground. For others, snow was not an option if you were from the South. Short sleeves and green grass could have been the weather standard. But tonight, for this snippet in time, this Christmas was a family tossed together once only. A onetime gift of the moment to be lived, remembered, and not repeated as a group, but perhaps as couples and maybe families in the future.

Christmas would be celebrated for whole week before Christmas in July. Even in dishwashing, where you would bring your dirty dishes, the staff would have a greeting for summer Christmas.

Christmas in July was a glue in many ways that bound the summer staff together in a way that could not be achieved any other way. Meaningful and joke gifts were exchanged; a more special gift was often exchanged later. It was presented to someone that was important in a person's life. This was a time of giving homemade Christmas cards and forever memories.

As the evening wore on, someone would start the record player with dance music. The chairs were shoved to the side, senior staff took their early-to-bed leave, and a seasonal dance began, which signaled the beginning of the close of the evening and the evening event.

At some point the celebration of Christmas in July spilled over to the guests. Perhaps it was the joyful spirit of staff that caught the attention of summer guests at this calendar date. Families planned vacations around July 25. The craft shop started presenting projects of the season. The Ad Building was decorated, each year more and more with seasonal decorations. Hyde Chapel became a summer statement of Christmas, and the message, well, it was the Christmas message.

I am sure there was more than curious confusion with conference guests and families seeing Christmas decorations midsummer. However, many times summer rules are not seasonal traditions. When you are only together for ninety days or so, you look for ways to pack a year or a lifetime of living into that time frame.

The next day, "Christmas Day," the staff tree was taken down, the pennants of colleges and universities were again placed on the walls, the holiday was now in the staff history books, and life returned to what was considered normal, whatever that was.

The staff had changed. There was a traditional softness in working interpersonal and especially personal relationships. Something unusual, magical, and unique culminated the night of Christmas in July. Nontraditional became traditional, Christmas hymns sung only once a year, now it seemed appropriate to sing year-round. The joy of giving was more than twice returned as there was more supportive give and less take. A greater picture was presented. The pallet of summer life was being painted differently for the rest of the summer.

The most wonderful time of the year was here, here for the duration of the summer. Occasionally you would hear staff greet each other a merry Christmas, and instant memory and laughter was present. Guests who were vacationing later in the summer had a quizzical look as to why that seasonal greeting in summer. The question was answered if asked, yet most of the time it was remembered as a fond greeting between staff.

The staff had been given a treasured gift, a gift of a memory of a time that a group of college students looking for summer work and fun experiencing a time in the Colorado Rockies came together as an extended family bound together by personal tradition for an event that continues to change the world.

It was, and had been, Christmas in July with the greatest present ever given to the world celebrated in a special way by God's children.

CHAPTER SIXTEEN

THE CHIMES AT HYDE CHAPEL

*Shout for joy to the L*ORD*, all the earth.*
Worship the Lord with gladness
come before him with joyful songs.
Know that the Lord is God. It is he who made us, and we
are his; we are his people, the sheep of his pasture.
Enter his gates with thanksgiving
and his courts with praise;
give thanks to him and praise his name.
For the Lord is good and his love endures forever
his faithfulness continues through all generations.
—Psalm 100

Sometimes you are in the right place at the exact moment of beauty. Often afternoon showers produce rainbows and this one over Hyde Chapel was no exception. This photo was taken recently; this is a tribute to all who worshiped, played the chimes and have met in this chapel. Photo by David Francis

At some time, someone or an entity thought it was a good idea to place electronic chimes in the bell tower of Hyde Chapel. The idea was to play them at opportune times, during church when needed, and at the end of the day just before or after the dinner hour. The amplification was strong enough to be heard across most of the lower area of the Y camp.

After the chimes, a gift from a church, were installed, the next step was creating a schedule of when, who, and what was to be played and what the duration of the "concert" would be.

You have to understand, God so loved the world that He didn't send a committee, and at this time the application of His grace was coming into focus. Maintenance had completed their job of installation. The testing was successful; the musical system worked. There was a switch that would allow either sanctuary only sound or outside and sanctuary sound. It seems that was always an electronic challenge as to whether the chimes were being heard outside.

Mom and a few others senior staff were selected as the musical chime committee to formulate and implement a plan. That is where the fun began. Anytime you get strong-willed people together, say three or more, you tend to have six or more opinions. For a while it was a verbal rodeo of direction and scheduling. Eventually, over time and after a few meetings, all details were worked out to the best agreement that could be made.

Because I was young, under my parents' direction, I was elected to go with Mom the nights she was to play three or four hymns. That was fine, because on the way home the Rustic Room with soft serve ice cream was there, and I reasoned I could cajole my need of a cold sweet calorie treat to Mom and get a big scoop of that delicacy. Didn't quite work that way all the time, but it did some, and that was a bonus I could live with.

Before the selected time on the chime schedule, Mom would look through the hymnal for a hymn friendly to the limited two active chime keyboard and a hymn that had not been played by one of the other "chimers," as I secretly called them. The process of selection would be completed over several days.

At the appointed time, hymnal in hand, keys secured to the chapel organ, and an attitude of anticipation mixed with a modicum of reverence, we would make our way to Hyde Chapel for this musical presentation that would last around ten minutes, per the agreement of the mighty three chimers.

Because vacuum tubes were the only way of amplification at that time in technology, you would arrive early enough to let the organ, which the chimes were attached to, warm up. That would take a few minutes, but it seemed like hours to me. All this happened after you got the key to unlock the organ, lights on to see the music selection, adjusted the organ bench, said a prayer that everything would work like planned and no notes would be missed or struck wrong (after all, the Y world was listening).

Before the chimes could be played, my assignment was to go outside of the chapel and listen for a note to ensure the bell tower speaker was broadcasting the clarion call of hymns. This task would require going in and out of the building several times as mother and son didn't quite communicate as well as should be. "I didn't hear anything," standard son reply. "I haven't played a note yet, go back outside and wait," parental reply.

I would dutifully go back outside, wait and wait, and wait some more, then the door of the chapel would open. It would be Mom inquiring if I heard anything, replying with a "no" from me and Mom was back inside trying again to broadcast musical notes to the world. The moment the music was to start was rapidly approaching. One didn't want to be late as the other two chimers would be listening, timing, and critiquing the performance, the power of pressure.

Sound outside heard, check; son inside reporting sound, check; hymnal on organ and hand on chime keyboard, double check. Let the chimes begin. And with reverence of duty, the nervous shaking of Mom's musical hands, the few hymns for a limited time would start. It was almost over before it started.

Mom was in her musical world, concentrating on the proper note for the precise musical length of time. I went outside to listen and watch people. With each note the softening of the day became more evident. People would stop and listen; conversations would give over to both people listening. You could sense a leisurely comfort of the soul as the chimes tolled out known hymns, "Faith of Our Fathers," "Holy, Holy, Holy." Note after note carried a signaling that the quiet part of the day was starting, even for a moment. Personal reflective time was offered through the electronic chimes high atop the bell tower.

Food had been prepared, consumed, dishes cleaned, and rocking chairs at the Ad Building along with the Adirondak Chairs occupied. The tall shadows of evening were starting to creep across the ground. The mountains were the last to witness direct sunlight. It was the beginning of the end of the day.

One more hymn and we would have completed our evening musical duty. Mom always held the last note a bit longer, her signal and signature that this part of the day was completed.

I would think back and be curious what it was like in a small town when our country was being formed. Back when the solidarity of religious freedom held a focal point in many families. I had read somewhere that the tolling of the church bell at the end of the day signaled just that. A time to stop, quit what you were doing, and focus on family.

The chimes of the Y held that responsibility, even if you didn't realize it. It was part of the evening rhythm as those extended shadows captured the evening light.

Soon campfires would be light, hay rides were being started, evening short walks completed, and pacing was slowing to the anticipation of a sleeping pace. Tomorrow would be another day. Tomorrow another volunteer on the chime schedule would take their place after carefully selecting what was to be presented across hill and valley. Mom would often sit on our porch where she could hear what was played. There would be a continual comment stream about the selection, the time the chimes started, and how long they were played. That was just Mom. She wanted to be at the right electronic professional level as the other musicians.

I know now she never realized she was the one who set the musical bar for this segment of time. It wasn't because she was the manager's wife; she simply did what was needed at the highest standard she could achieve. She was a gifted musician. That is why I often heard her practicing on our little electronic organ at the cabin. She wanted to be ready, ready to present a small space between heaven and earth with an electronic set of chimes.

I realized decades later the hymn "It Is Well with My Soul" was as special to me as it was to her. Somehow, the hymn's title and listening to it being tolled across hill and valley did make it well with your soul.

PART III

1956–1965

CHAPTER SEVENTEEN

MOUNTAINSIDE PURCHASE, CHECK WRITING ON A CAR FENDER

Let this be written for a future generation, that a people not yet created may praise the Lord.
—Psalm 102:18

Mountainside Lodge stands as a tall statement of many people's commitment for preservation and family memories. It is listed on the Colorado and National Register of Historic Places, thus keeping history available.

There are many landmark moments in a person's life that turn into an everlasting memory. This circumstance involved my father, an automobile ride, and the end and the beginning of a new chapter of a lodge on a mountaintop.

"Hop in," he said. "I want you to go with me on an errand." An errand, I thought, what is with that? I was not asked to go on a lot of errands, but everyone I did go on was an adventure. No doubt I would not be disappointed.

I got in and looked around for a hint, for some type of clue as to the errand we were doing. I didn't see anything I could relate to an answer as to what we were doing. The only item of information I saw was a notebook that you would keep papers in on the bench seat of car. Wonder what is in there, I thought and didn't give it another thought. When you got to go with Walt, you didn't question; you just did.

We didn't turn toward town but traveled on the camp roads up a dusty mountain road. I had been part way up here, but a ten-year-old can only venture so far. We were going past places new to me, excitement built as to our destination. This was an adventure, and I felt the anticipation in my soul that this would be a landmark day.

I kept looking for our journey's end. We could not go too far, I reasoned, as dirt mountain roads could not go that far. Besides, dad didn't like his car to get too dusty, and this was a dirt road doing its best to change the color of the vehicle.

As we traveled, I saw a large log building on the side of the mountain standing out as if the structure was, could be, our destination. As we traveled toward the building and the hewn logs, the four-story structure continued to grow in size and stature to the mountain.

We passed through a rock gate-like entrance signaling perhaps a property line for the building that continued to rise in size and stature as we traveled closer and closer. The silent statement of what I know to be Mountainside Lodge was ahead, and we stopped short of reaching the lodge.

Dad had not talked at all on the way up; that was usual. Driving was his silent and thinking time. As a family, Mom and I respected the silence as well as did the radio of the car, for it was seldom on.

We stopped, parked, and occupied the dusty road. Somehow, I knew this was a time to watch, listen, and not forget. Something special was going to happen. We sat in the car for a moment or two. Dad was looking at the papers in the notebook. His eyes held a look of excitement and a look of sadness too. I wondered about both.

From where we sat in the road, one could see all the way down the valley to the town of Estes Park. I wondered what you could see from the rooftop of the lodge.

My thoughts were interrupted when Dad opened the door of the car and more dust migrated in. The car is going to get washed, I thought. Maybe I can help. I decided to tag along. Most of the time, sitting in the car or waiting at a table was my role. The silent child along for the ride, but not today. Something was going to happen, and I wanted to be right there in the moment.

By the time I got out of the car and to the driver's side, Dad was talking to another man in an understanding but official corporate voice. Dad's car had large, wide fenders, and the hood was close to flat and could be used as a writing surface. The notebook was still closed on the hood of the car.

"This is a good but sad day," the stranger said. "I am glad the old gal is going to be a part of the Y and not something else." What's that relate to? I wondered. "The kids sure have enjoyed having camp here," the stranger said. Dad let him talk. His eyes roamed across the property, taking in what was going to be close to last looks of the property.

"Well." That was the signal word from Dad that it was time to move on, make a decision, and close a meeting. "I have a paper for you to sign and a check for you." I realized this was a selling-and-pur-chasing moment and where we were standing was going to belong to the Y camp now. That is why it was so quiet; the owner was the only person here. What had been a kids' summer camp was over. There would be no more camps and no more kids this season or any other season for that matter.

Dad opened the notebook. It was like the opening of a vault, no ceremony but a ceremony. The stranger, now becoming former youth camp director and owner, was handed some papers. "I guess this is it," he said. "Might as well sign the papers and go from there." There, where was there? I wondered. There was the finality in his voice. Near was the end. There was soon to be somewhere else.

Dad stood silently as he, now not the owner, signed the papers and handed them back to Dad. The two directors, one of a youth camp, the other of the Y, shuffled papers back and forth to each person. Papers and a deed to Dad and a check to the stranger.

"Still glad you got the property. Take care of her, she holds lots of memories, lots of memories." You could hear resignation and yet a whole lot of comfort in his voice as he knew Mountainside would be taken care of, preserved, and protected. And now another life awaited this mountaintop structure.

"Thank you. The Y will take good care of her," Dad said as he shook the now-former owner's hand. They held each other's gaze for a long understanding moment as the transfer of ownership was completed.

"Well," Dad said, the signal to move on. "You are welcome any time to come and visit, the camp and the lodge will be here." The stranger nodded in understanding, but I felt he would not be back. Sometimes memories are best kept as memories. Seasons change; so do people. Memories of accomplishments past are best kept as just that. The future changes; the past stays the same. Like water and oil, there is no mixing.

We got back in the car and started down the road minus a check but with a title to a new addition to the Y.

"This was a tough day for him. He is a good youth camp director," Dad said. After a pause, Dad talked about all the kids who contain memories of a week, maybe two, at Mountainside. The activities and the stables where we met the stranger. The hiking trails leading into the national park.

"It is hard to make a youth camp go when you are so far off the road." I listened. "He really did try to keep the place going."

"What will happen now to the place?" I asked. There was a long pause, and I saw Dad carefully crafting his answer.

"The lodge will make a great place for family reunions. A place where they can be all together with no one else in the building."

Families—that was what this trip was about, a legacy place to weave together that unique and special bond of people loving each other. That was a bit like a youth camp with adults and kids both allowed, I thought.

The errand was just about over. We stopped in front of our summer cabin. Dad was anxious to get back to his office and the next task at hand, whatever that might be. The time taken to pass the ownership from one era to another had only taken an hour, but the ageless offering of protection was timeless.

I knew I had been witness to something bigger than I would realize at the time. I also realized I now was a child observer of a precious part of history. I also decided I wanted to be a larger part of Mountainside. She was like a big sister to me now, and I wanted to visit as often as I could. My goal was to work there doing what I could to be a part of what I was privileged to have witnessed on that dusty road high on a mountain.

I got out of the car. "Thanks for taking me, it was neat," I told Dad. He just nodded and said he would see me at dinner. I knew something would come up, and that was likely not to happen as planned.

The notebook was on the seat of the car, different now as it held the legal future of the lady of the mountain, protected within the borders of the Y. Protected because the legacy of loving would continue there with relative travelers driving up a dusty road to almost the top of a mountain to bond and bind together families. They will have their memories, but I have mine, watching two people keeping a log legacy safe.

CHAPTER EIGHTEEN

Big Jim and the Potato War

Would they argue with useless words, with speeches that have no value?

—*Job 15:3*

I don't know how Big Jim got his name. I do know Big Jim was huge. He towered above many, and his wife, Bertha, was shorter but just as mighty. You did what they said and then some.

Dad always said there are many ways to judge a cook; one way is by their size. If that is true, then in Big Jim's case, he was a gourmet cook at the Y camp.

Jim and Bertha came on staff when there was a food crisis, there was not a cook to be found, and people needed to eat. I don't recall where Big Jim came from. Back East, I was told, but the past was not the present, and that settled the conversation.

Big Jim instructing kitchen staff on the proper placement, size and speed as to serving meals. Note the stack of dishes, meals were once served this way with staff transporting food on large oval trays, which sometimes proved there was gravity in the dining room.

When Big Jim came into the kitchen, you could always locate him as he was larger than you would expect from the average cook. His presence alone was enough to get your attention, then his voice came into play. Just simply listening was enough to reveal his location in a noisy kitchen. Big Jim could bark orders from the serving line to the prep area and across the dishwasher. He was the king of the kitchen, and Bertha was his queen.

Big Jim would don his apron, and he would have to use all the apron cord to tie that white uniform on, then he would get his chef's hat, and he was ready to prepare for the day. Big Jim worked all three meals alongside Bertha, who was in charge of the bakery. They were a team.

Big Jim and Bertha always had a nice and new car; that was important to them. Presentation was everything, from the car to the way food was placed on the meal plate. Once, there was a discussion about three or four small round potatoes. Big Jim said one figure;

Bertha hand another figure in mind. As this discussion continued to progress, an employee was standing in the serving line just about frozen in time. He was assigned the task of serving this food item. The servers holding their food trays were in a row with their trays at the ready. The trays could be used as shields, and I don't doubt this was being considered. The rest of the kitchen staff was locked into place as Big Jim and his foodmate worked out the "three potato, four potato" details. John simply stood there with two spoons, one with Big Jim's amount and the other with Bertha's suggestion of the amount. Big Jim said his amount, and John would lift that serving spoon, then Bertha would respond, and the other serving spoon would rise to the statement.

One spoon, then the other, it seemed this dialogue went on for several minutes. The kitchen world was at a standstill until the potato crisis count would be resolved, and that brought a new meaning to the term "hunger games." About in the middle of the emotional duologue, Big Jim and Bertha noticed what John (the potato server) was doing, time to redirect to John. Down went the serving spoons, and John stood there, hands behind his back, head down. His fingers were crossed as the situation took on a different direction.

Big Jim's look of fire in his eyes started to soften. Bertha was not far behind in relinquishing the great potato count. Jim could laugh, and when he did, he shook like a Jell-O earthquake. The laughter started slowly in a chuckle sort of way and then a crescendo into a full belly laugh. Well, this got Bertha giggling too. John now raised his head to the food heavens in silent thanks.

I don't recall the potato number on the serving, but what I do recall is the instant love of Big Jim and Bertha, laughing at themselves as they looked around the kitchen seeing everyone watching, wondering, and waiting to serve those in the dining room. John started to dish out the potatoes, three on one plate, four on the other. Problem solved, hunger abated, compromise reached.

Big Jim, Bertha and staff serving Sunday Dinner in the Pine Room another YMCA tradition for guests. Pictured are Garland and Helen Matthews, staff counselors along with other staff and guests.

CHAPTER NINETEEN

THE ART OF EGG CRACKING

May the grace of the Lord Jesus Christ, and the love of God, and the fellowship of the Holy Spirit be with you all.

—*2 Corinthians 13:14*

Cracking eggs is really no big deal, until you are told you need to bust open enough eggs for two thousand people and each person gets about two and a half eggs. Do the math, five thousand of those oblong white orbs, or 416 dozen! Now the fun begins.

When you are on kitchen staff, you learn to adapt to any situation, from cooking, serving, cleaning, even cracking a plethora of eggs for the breakfast meal.

Egg cracking is a task for the afternoon crew, a duty that does allow you to sit down, but that is about all. You generally grab a chair and a ten-gallon tub and find a comfortable place on the loading dock porch so you can watch the world go by because you will be here cracking up for several hours.

Shucking corn, like the process of egg cracking, an opportunity for social interaction in the kitchen. This was also a long chore, but well worth the taste.

On each side of the aluminum tub you place a stack of egg racks that you retrieved from the walk-in cooler. In front of you is a receptacle for the shells, at least the ones that are not part of the secret ingredients of the mixture of eggs.

There is a mechanical rhythm to this task of egg cracking. When you get good, you can use each hand to break open the shell, split the capsule apart, dump the ingredients, and toss the remains.

Crack, crack, split, split, dump, toss, toss is the cadence you are working to achieve. Like a volleyball game of continuing tossing the ball across the net, you continue, one egg at a time. A skill needs to be developed, and part of that skill is becoming ambidextrous in your busting of egg. There is a specific place you need to aim for to get the perfect splitting of the shell that is close but not exactly on the circumference. You need to aim a bit to the left on your right and right on your left so you have some leverage with your fingers to split the orb and dump the ingredients. If you hit the exact middle, there is no leverage, and you then require two hands to complete the task. Only rookies do that. We are not rookies; we are first-line, professional egg destroyers. Hear us cackle, crack, and cluck.

It is also a time to people-watch as staff and guests walk by. I often wonder if they think this egg cracking army is making any progress. At least there is some knowledge as to what is for breakfast. Crack, crack, each hand working in synchronization to the other. Split, split, plop, plop, the beat goes on.

Of course, at some point, a half a shell will decide it does not want to depart from is duty to contain its contents and in the eggs, it descends. Egg shells are supposed to float. Some do; most don't. The cauldron of goo captures the shell and sends it somewhere hiding behind a yellow yoke. Small pieces of calcium you can ignore, but a large piece, you need to retrieve the bandit. That is why you wear short sleeves and should be wearing long gloves.

This is when you look around to see who is looking because you are diving your arm into egg goo up to your elbows. One would question about using a spoon or something to retrieve the calcium convict, but spoons don't have the opportunity of feeling, and there is a bit of chasing that will go on. So, in your arm goes, and the search begins ever so delicately until you get the shell, and out your hand and arm come, dripping egg white. Not the healthiest of procedure, but what the heck; the goop will be scrambled (that should count for some sanitation), cooked (again sanitation), placed in a warming oven, and served. Sanitation times three.

By now your hands are tired from the cracking. You are cold (remember, the eggs were in the cooler chilled to a hypothermic temperature) even though it is a warm summer day. The racks that were stacked on each side of you are lowered to nothing but cardboard, and around you are vats full of cracked eggs. You will never look at scrambled eggs the same way again.

There is a certain feeling of accomplishment completing this task. You and the others have decimated five thousand eggs, created more space in the cooler, talked about almost everything while some guest have paused to watch the cracking experts, and during that time nary a shell escaped the trash by taking a side trip.

You are reminded how heavy the egg cartons were when you attempt to lift and move the heavy vat of eggs. It takes two people to lift the potential soon-to-be-scrambled breakfast concoction.

A whisk large enough to beat and scramble the eggs with is used to mix breakfast, but this task takes strength and skill to integrate the two ingredients (don't count the small pieces of shell) into one. You smash and stir like you are auditioning for a part as the cauldron mixer in *The Wizard of OZ*. Each vat gets the same treatment. Each egg cracker is part of the mixing team. Soon all is mixed together, ready for the morning crew to use.

Everything that is food goes back to the cooler; the rest, landfill somewhere someplace. The task is complete, the goo crew is done, but the dumb jokes continue. The puns abound from the others on the kitchen crew. "This is the time to crack up, bad yoke, egg you on and white on . . . when you are done yellow . . ." We don't respond. We have heard them all, sitting on the loading dock from those who walked by. We will again be cracking eggs, hearing the same lines again, but the conversation about colleges, education majors, brothers, sisters, parents is the verbal glue that keeps us volunteering to do this task. The art of cracking multiple eggs is often not about the task but the conversation and recognizing what shell you are in and developing a course, a plan, goals to break free and find a direction that suits just you. One can learn much from an egg-cracking conversation.

CHAPTER TWENTY

THE COOKOUT SHELTER AND WATERMELONS

Whatever you do, work at it with all your heart, as working for the Lord, not for human masters.
—Colossians 3:23

Cooking outside brings its own accumulation of challenges. When you plan a cookout for a conference group of two thousand, planning and procedure are often at opposite ends of the spectrum. For a young know-it-all high school student, a cookout should not be a stretch, or so I thought.

What is there to cook for a couple thousand people? I thought. The cookout crew and I would be outdoors embracing nature. We would not be in a hot kitchen on a summer day. Clean up would be easy. There would be all disposable plates and utensils. I figured this job would be easy.

When you get your mind set on something, you talk about it. The other staff who had been at the cookout listened, and I thought it unusual that there was little or no comment about how easy this work assignment would be.

The menu was simple, small steaks, corn on the cob, a mixed salad, baked beans, and for dessert, watermelon. What was there to stress over? That is where I was wrong.

Transporting food for two thousand is a task that requires several staff to accomplish. Consider the steaks. Each steak is eight ounces. That is a half a ton you must move from a walk-in refrigerator to a delivery van and then move once again for the third time to the staging area at the cookout; half a ton turns into a ton and a half. Corn on the cob is no walk in the cornfield either. Box after box needs to be transported, hauled the same way. Boxes are stacked like pillars of corny cardboard to the top of the food van. Baked beans are in large number ten cans; that amounts to a lot of cans in boxes. Salad just simply takes up lots of space. The watermelon—well, now the real fun begins. I found out those melons were to be my assignment, and to familiarize myself with them, I loaded carton after carton into the already filled vehicle. Finally, all the disposable plates, cups, plasticware, napkins, and cooking gear needed to go too. Getting everything to the cookout shelter was completed with several trips. Working for the summer at the cookout started to lose it luster of laziness very quickly.

The cookout shelter consists of a large covered open-air building with picnic tables and a food prep and serving area where we would serve a high-altitude Colorado Rockies meal. There was no commercial dishwasher there; used serving pans and utensils would go back to the main kitchen, and we were responsible for washing them as the other shifts were over. This assignment was quickly becoming a food purgatory of placement for me. I was wondering why I thought this was going to be a good idea.

Other kitchen staff who were considered senior staff were assigned premium duties like grilling the steaks, heating the Boston baked beans, tossing the salad, and cooking the corn; these were the preferred jobs. I was a runner helping get the needed supplies to the person requesting them. I had completely forgotten about the watermelon, but apparently, the rest of the crew had not forgotten.

Cookouts were a social event. Families would meet other families from across the USA and a lifetime friendship would be forged. Note the watermelon on the right… author's food assignment area.

For a few hours, we prepared the food, and soon it was getting close to serving time. Guests were arriving and visiting with each other, then it happened. All the boxes we had unloaded of watermelons were at the end of the serving line, and I was told my job was to half, quarter, and slice the watermelon for the entire two thousand hungry, watermelon-craving group. That is when I knew I had been hijacked to food preparation prison. There was box upon box of green oblong blimp-looking "things" that needed to be quickly cut into proper shapes and sizes for the group. On the table were several knives. Because of the many knives, I wondered if I was the only one on this task, and looking at the size of the table, that question was answered—it was only me. Me, the melons, several knives, I was doomed.

One of the senior summer staff members showed me how to quickly cut the watery melon as juice accumulated on the table and on the concrete floor. I was instructed how to place the sliced quarters in a serving pan and smile while this chore was being performed.

There is something about watermelon, the sticky red liquid and the inevitably annoying flying insects that are not attractive to the person doing the surgical procedure of dissecting the object. The hungry, dessert-craved guests are unaware of this force of nature, but when you are the cutter, you are in the middle of a small flying insect circus. I didn't realize how much bees love the sweetness of watermelons and how frustrating flies can be. With the buzzing around you as you carry out your appointed task, each cut brings you closer to knowing this is a "special" way to serve a guest.

You cut, swat, cut, swing your knife around, trying to keep a smile on your face and the flies off your exposed arms. The sweet juices of the orb are flowing off the table into or close to a catch pail, yet you are becoming more and more covered with liquid watermelon evidence.

With each melon, you think you are closer to the end of this experience, and then you remember you asked to be on the cookout crew and this crew will be repeating this whole process of loading, unloading, cooking, watermelon dissection three times a week for over two months. Joy just abounds in your little watermelon-cutting heart. What were you thinking, or were you thinking?

Finally, the last melon is diced up, the hungry horde is moving on, and you are covered with the sticky evidence of many now-gone watermelons, except for the exoskeletons of this gourd.

Cleaning the cookout shelter is quick and fairly easy. Most of the work is accomplished with a garden hose and a high-pressure spray nozzle. You consider becoming a target in this phase of the process as the flies and bees continue to follow you like the pied piper of Melonville.

At this juncture, one realizes they will be taking a rather long, use-all-the-hot-water kind of shower, probably with your shoes on as they are also a friend of the crawling and flying insect population. Seems ants like watermelon juice too. You have sliced your way into history, cutting enough pieces for the hungry two thousand. It has been a learning experience and also an accomplishment.

Part of the anticipation at a cookout was receiving steak cooked over an open grill, outside and getting it hot right off the grill. Most groups would ask for a cookout –a high-altitude tradition.

Dinner is now served to the cookout crew, each of us wearing a certain badge of recognition of the duty we performed. The grillers of steak smelled and looked like a poster boy for charcoal. "Corn on the cob" people were adorned with some of the fixings of corn on the cob, they smelled like butter. "Boston baked beans" servers were the cleanest; they also had the longest serving spoons. Salad people were clean too; they were a shirt-tale relative to the bean crew. Me, well I looked and smelled like a whole field of melons. My arms were as sticky as fly paper, and the flies were there to prove it. My apron was a watermelon color; even under my fingernails were little gifts from—as far as I was concerned—the forbidden fruit.

I used to like watermelon. I was developing a rapid distaste of the fruit, especially knowing I was going to be doing this task for the duration of the summer. One could only hope for torrential rainstorms and cookouts being canceled. Then I remembered we were under cover; weather didn't matter. The cookout would go on.

Looking around again at the cookout crew, I sensed something unique and special was present here. We were from different places in the country, none of us from the same learning establishment. Each of us had dreams and goals, some goals more defined than others, but nevertheless, we were placed together to serve for the summer, watermelon and all. That was the common goal.

I wondered who would become what—teacher, lawyer, doctor, mechanic. What did God have in mind for each of us? Would some get married and have a large family? Some would choose career over family, but I sensed God had a special and unique plan for each of us, even if we didn't know what that was right now. Sometimes the conversation around the picnic table would reveal a caveat of information about the future of an individual if you were quick enough to catch the phrase. We all had something to give, something to share, something to tell about ourselves. No judgment, lots of kidding, and even more love as the summer would move on.

The tall shadows of evening dusk were starting to grow, signaling the end of another day of service to guests from many different cities, states, and countries. We were a food service team, a meat-cooking, corn-on-the-cob-boiling, salad-and-bean-tossing unit with a kid in high school learning the definition of food service work.

As we turned off the lights and locked the back room of the cookout shelter, we concluded we had completed a good thing this evening. It wasn't just serving a great meal. It was not just the team working together. It was far, far more than that. We had become servants to people we didn't know, individuals who didn't know us, but all of us bound together by the common need of food and fellowship.

I thought this will be a long summer sectioning watermelon (no one else was even close to volunteering for this fine task). I will be an attraction for flying irritations and will take on the fragrance of Ode de Watermelon. But in spite of it all, I will be serving not only watermelon but an outdoor cookout memory with a crew of a few who will be serving many. That was good enough for me. Good enough to look forward, somewhat, to being on the cookout crew.

One thing I decided as we all got in the van holding on to whatever we could for the short ride back to the main kitchen is this experience of slicing watermelon told me I would never again embrace the taste of watermelon, and that was OK.

CHAPTER TWENTY-ONE

WORKING AT MOUNTAINSIDE LODGE IN 1960

Serve wholeheartedly, as if you were serving the Lord, not people.

—Ephesians 6:7

Mountainside Lodge, with all its history and memories, is a unique place. It is as if the lodge has always been there, a place where the seasonal winds move around the building and oftentimes through the old log siding that comprise this grandfather of lodges.

It was built by George Wiard from 1919 to 1921 as a retreat for Presbyterian ministers and families. Dr. Timothy Stone was the original owner; however, the lodge has been host to not only ministers but was a speakeasy in the twenties during prohibition and also a boys' camp in the summer before purchased by the YMCA of the Rockies in 1956.

Every room is unique and diverse like the lodge, each room with its own personality. As you walk up the fifteen hand-picked rock steps to the quiet, yet wide hand-hewn front door, you sense you are entering a time capsule of sorts. A contrivance that allows you the opportunity of new memories, particularly those you will create while you are in the comfortable arms of Mountainside.

Mountainside is now a retreat, from a past service of many occupations; some of the lodge's past have questionable histories. Yet this log dwelling can become an old friend you come home to many times, even if this is your first time here, but you must allow this friendship to happen.

The lodge is placed halfway up a small, but impressive mountain named Emerald Mountain. It is nestled on the side of the mountain, a space that was conceivably created just for this edifice. Each room has its own spectacular and personal view of the world. Some look out on the mountain, others across the valley, and others are cloistered among the swaying of the pine trees, which embrace Mountainside with the ever passing of the wind. The sound you hear is perhaps the consciousness of the lodge and the mountain, living together, yet separately.

Working at the lodge offers another perspective of the art of living. You become part of the internal historical structure, if you will, of a four-story log building, built with loving dedication to God as a place of rest, solace, reflection, and hospitality to all who pass through the entrance of the lodge.

The road to Mountainside winds up Emerald Mountain like a dusty tributary looking for a destiny of a destination that ends at the massive lodge's rock doorsteps. One doesn't know or even realize how many individuals have climbed these steps, entered in the large structure with its large supportive ceiling beams, looked at the horizontal structure of logs, and seen the views from the now-aged rippled single-pane windows.

The mornings are chilly as we load already an ample warm breakfast prepared at the kitchen at the main camp down below for the resident guests at Mountainside. The lodge kitchen crew will travel in the old wood-paneled 51 Chevy station wagon that will labor and grind its way up the pockmarked-many-times one-lane dirt road to Mountainside. You can smell the chill of clear air only to be redirected and interrupted by the aroma of eggs, bacon, and biscuits. We will make coffee at Mountainside, but cooking is out of the question due to the age of the lodge and fire hazards, and the fact that this group of summer staff has not a clue how to prepare food for fifty or so. We are food servants, there to serve for the summer, one guy and three gals from three different colleges and universities, all as one team, serving a reunion of families.

As we get in the old tired Chevy and close the vault-like doors, a journey we have made all summer is about to begin again for the first time. With protest, the old car starts, and we are on our way, grinding gears and hoping the brakes hold out on the trip back down. Now mixes the odor of the crisp clear morning air along with an engine that will overheat only to be accented by the gathering of dust as we travel a path to serve. Extra spices for the morning meal never hurt, or so we reason.

Slowly we climb the upward for miles to the log lady in the sky. This road with its curves, dips, and dust has become the only link to Mountainside. About halfway on our upward travels, the lodge appears in a welcome posture that seems to tell you the journey will again be presenting a memory worth a lifetime to the travelers and the guests and staff.

We pass through the stone gate entrance that was built when the lodge had been a retreat for Reverend Timothy Stone. Gone now were the barriers of the previous owners; the three-strand barbwire fence, part of the opening, gone with the ravages of time and atrophy of not being needed anymore.

The Chevy is down to first gear with the engine protesting the final climb to the lodge. The food has been seasoned with a great deal of sloshing, bouncing, and dust of course—three secret ingredients no cook could or would be willing to match or use for that matter.

As we pull into the parking lot, the dust that chased us up the mountain fully catches us, surrounding us, causing us to cough and sneeze along with being the last final seasoning for our morning meal. The dusty air will soon clear. We have arrived at 9,900 feet above sea level and have gained over 2,000 feet in altitude from the kitchen down below.

What was large and important down the mountain seems insignificant and unimportant when you are close to the mountaintop. We are as high as we can reach in a vehicle; the rest, if we require a loftier experience, will require hiking, but that is not what we are here for.

Each of us carries breakfast seasoned with that road dust to the upstairs kitchen. The hungry guests will soon start awakening with the aroma of the morning sounds and smells of breakfast being readied for serving. We travel bringing substance in the form of breakfast, yet that is of no consequence now as we enter the lower cavern of Mountainside. The lower ground floor was used for staff sometime long ago; now they are vacant, with stories untold and secrets within. Getting to the kitchen requires traversing a rickety, unlit stairway with a trapdoor at the top that requires a delicate balancing act of pushing up, holding a large warm pan of food, and keeping your balance all at the same time. (I keep thinking this procedure could be an Olympic sport.)

Pushing open the ceiling trapdoor, we are greeted with a curiousness of what we will find on the other side. Mountainside Lodge hosts lots of secrets, and the creaking of the stairs and moaning of the trapdoor adds to the mystery of something not known. You will always wonder what awaits you on the other side; that is part of the adventure.

Will the lodge hostess be there, waiting? Are the ovens lit and warm, ready to keep breakfast at a decent temperature? Will the water heater be working, or is boiling water going to be part of the workday? Lighting the gas stove, like the ovens, requires a certain amount of survival skill. Appliances reliable in their day now are in question as to reliability and safety but are needed to keep breakfast warm.

Slowly one opens the trapdoor in the hope that no one is standing on it or close to it. Seeing a floor move in the early morning light and not being quite awake will get you awake in a heartbeat. The door floor hinges creak with the warning this is again another uncounted time the floor will give passage to a new event in the making. The counterweight of the door hurls against the wall, startling you into thinking something sinister, something unknown is lurking close by. Dark halls, creaky floors, and a rumor of a dark history will do that to you. The warmth of the kitchen embraces you along with the aroma of fresh brewed coffee. The ovens and stove have granted another day in your favor.

You now are tasked with getting the rest of the pans of food up the open stairway. It is time to prepare the rest of the morning meal. We all have our own chores, such setting the tables in the dining room (need to wipe them off first; dust has slept there). Another chore is getting the food situated in the ovens, and one staff member is off looking for the host and hostess to see if there are any special instructions for the day and to also thank them for starting the ovens and the coffee.

We work for two bosses, the cook down at the main kitchen, who has certain requirements, and the host and hostess at Mountainside, who circumvent those main kitchen policies as often as necessary. We listen to the direction of the host and hostess. They are here; others are there down below. It all works out.

The aroma of the morning is accented with the tempting scent of breakfast as the guests recognize breakfast is about to be served, which triggers the guests to start looking for reasons to come into the kitchen to "help." The mountain atmosphere requires the overconsumption of more coffee for everyone; you oblige. This also seems to be the case with food also. We are ready, tables set, food in serving pans; let the morning feast begin. Places for staff and places for guests, the world is in order.

Sunlight cascades into the dining room, accenting that the day is now beginning. Wind rustles the leaves of the aspen trees outside. We keep the windows open, it is the sound of nature, the sound of a timeless presence of others who have dined here. The guests come into the sunny dining room choosing who they will dine with. Because Mountainside is used for family reunions, families tend to move around changing dining partners at each meal.

Some of the relatives have never met part of their heritage. The bonding of cousins meeting cousins for the first time is instant, so seating changes, like life. The amount of conversation is continuous as people become family and more familiar with their legacy, both past, present, and what will be the future. Like roots of a tree discovered by unearthing the ground, relative roots are discovered, followed and joined in the forest that we call family. The past is appreciated more; the meaning of family is solidified. In the table conversation individuals become a part of a greater, larger family. Adults and children recognize there is a not-so-distant love that is ignited in a reunion, and another group of memories are seared in the hearts of many.

Soon breakfast is over, and this time becomes a memory of conversation, food, and a large consumption of coffee.

Over breakfast, the conversation turns to who will be going where, what cars will be available for hikes, shopping, the bookworms tell of their current read, and an exchange of history continues to flow from the faucet of memories, turning the information into understanding of relative commitment.

At some point information of a distant cousin is shared who is not present and a promise to catch them up is made; now they are included in a remote, but loving way. Information about another relative is shared, a memory confirmed about a great-grandparent, which leads to another conversation about an additional family member.

As people continue to talk, we, the staff, have the task of cleaning up the dining room. Several of the guests pitch in, which results in including staff in family planning conversations. We become honorary family. We haven't asked guests to help with the cleaning of the dining room, but this occurs because of the sense of unity Mountainside fosters to all that vacation and work there.

The dishes are not light or even close to dainty. They are, like the lodge, survivors. Heavy ceramic plates, cups, etc., that do not match in pattern. Coffee mugs you could use as a paperweight in a hurricane and serving dishes that would make a good foundation for a structure.

The dishwasher in the kitchen was added as an afterthought to the rest of the building. The floor slopes down a few inches every foot or so as this part of the kitchen was built on what had been a roof. No matter, the sink, worktable, and dish shelves are level; even the chairs have been adjusted so you can sit level. You always are reminded of the fact there are two diminutions of "level" the first time you stack dishes on the storage shelves as one will aim high or low incorrectly depending on whether you are standing up on the high side or on your tiptoes on the down side of the shelf. I don't know how many times someone has placed dishes too high or too low, but judging from the dent marks in the wood this would indicate this has happened more than could be counted.

Washing dishes for up to fifty guests is when teams are built; a good dishwashing effort can clean plates with their hands in extremely hot soapy water, "rack 'em," and run the plates, saucers, cups, and such through the "dishwasher" (which really only rinses them), and be ready for the next rack by the time the cylinder water machine has finished its cycle.

Silverware was another problem; it has to be hand cleaned, rinsed, dried, and sorted. This takes time, so the flatware is relegated to the last task. Here is when conversations that are shared, fears, joys, goals, plans, and a growth of friendship comes into focus from of the drying/sorting time. You can sit there at the level table on the sloped floor and share your thoughts and feelings bound by flatware and wet dish towels as you dry the unmatched patterns of knives, forks, and spoons.

It is as if time has slowed, but increased in quality. You sit at that long kitchen table, picking either the lower on one end, which matches the window, or the other end where it is warmer because of the "dishwasher" and the heat it offers on a mountain summer day. There is the view of the mountains, snow-covered peaks waiting to be climbed, and the mountain breeze accented by the sounds of blue jays barking out commands of "Feed me, the feeders are empty." Then the crows have their opinion, although you never quite figure out what they want, except to make more noise than the blue jays.

Conversations circumvent a myriad of topics, school, family, what event is next when you are done with your shift. The subject of parents regularly comes up; it is rough to raise your parents when you are away for the summer of a lifetime. Not to worry. The parents and siblings are coming out, and you can't wait to show them what you do in an old lodge with secrets, memories, and a sloped kitchen floor. It seems that floor seems to level the outlook of life one utensil at a time as you are drying them.

Soon, but not soon enough, it seemed you were finished with the kitchen chores. All flatware and dishes, including the drudgery of pots and pans, were done; everything is lined up on the proper shelves and in placed in bins. Like a silent ceramic and silver army waiting to do battle to protect the hunger of the guests when this unique army is called into action at another time, which is not too far off, and the process repeats itself once again.

Most of the guests have gone for the day. The remaining few guests who stay around are either in their rooms, perhaps sitting in the log-hewn lobby with its fireplace or on one of the many decks, just taking in a Colorado day. The few guests who remain and staff are on their own. Some are wandering around the mountain that they believe they own perhaps for only a week in their lifetime, but for now, it is theirs.

We "own" the lodge now. Mostly void of guests, the lodge continues to be full of sounds of floors creaking, wind through a partially opened window or door. They are the noises the log structure makes as it takes a rest from humans. Sometimes you can hear the footfall of people above you, the scrapping of a chair, even the sound of water in the old exposed pipes. Occasionally the peaceful sound of a broom sweeping is accented by the outside chorus of chipmunks scurrying for what substance they can find. You work alone only to be interrupted by the lodge sounds and your thoughts.

Perhaps one would make believe that the lodge is your possession, your home. Then history creeps in to your thoughts. History of when Mountainside was a haven for gamblers during prohibition, then later a boys' camp with a horse stable, basketball courts, and other trappings of a youth camp. What stories the rooms could tell, but silent as the rooms are, one can make up for the quiet by creating stories of your own.

As you make up the beds, remember to miter the corners, and when you clean the bathrooms, knock first—always knock. Are there new towels, washcloths? Gather the dirty laundry and get this part of your work day completed. This is too far for housekeeping to come up, so we the kitchen crew are now the appointed housekeeping crew. We don't mind, another reason to linger at the mountaintop.

We are the sole providers of service to the lady on the mountain. We are simply the Mountainside crew.

As all the chores are done, there is time again for another opportunity to talk to each other. However, it is not like the silverware time. This time is reserved for a different conversation. The main group decision to be decided is, are we staying here until the afternoon, or do we go back down to the main camp? Traveling back down means a dose of valley reality, not mountain solace. There will be personal errands and a chance, a very good chance, we will be pressed into service in the main kitchen for an hour or so; that is unless we can park our mechanical wonder of a station wagon without being detected. We know the muffler will probably give us away. Staying on the mountain means a chance for rest or getting a board game going. It also means we can pretend we are guests for a few minutes or hours. We realize the bulk of the guests will be back midafternoon, and we will also have to get the evening meal, but for now, the time and the lodge is ours. Ours to allow Mountainside to embrace us and us to emotionally hug the lodge. There are places we can go to and not be disturbed. So for now, the answer is, we stay, hide away; this is our time, our special time.

We knew before the question was presented that we would stay. That is what we do all the time, and the main kitchen supervisors don't ever seem to catch on. Perhaps they think we are slow workers. For now, we own Mountainside.

I am drawn to what was the preacher's study located behind the fireplace in the lobby. This rock-hewn room has windows to the ceiling and is cloistered in its individuality. I can picture Dr. Stone studying here, dialoging with other men of the cloth, or just looking at the beauty of nature that can be seen from the expanse of windows. Half of the wall in this room is are rocks, not logs like the rests of Mountainside. One cannot help but see the striking difference from log to rock and the statement it makes: "Upon this rock, I will build my house." The floor is rock and not so even. The ledge where rock meets window is wide enough for reading material. It is the definition of a room with a view as the Rocky Mountains are in sight from anywhere in the room.

What I like is the small door that leads to the outside seating area. The door is not over five feet tall. Why is that? I wonder. Then the answer comes to me: one humbles himself entering God's natural kingdom, because you have to stoop down to exit what man has made with God's provision to see what God has created. Nice, Dr. Stone, well designed.

The study is devoid of any furniture. Minimal is a good description of the study, but I think many decisions and sermons were crafted in this space behind the fireplace. I don't know of any world-shaking directives that came from this room, but I can see that this room was the foundational room of Mountainside, as said "built upon a rock," and this, to me, is where it all began. If you are quiet, you can sense God's presence in this room of study and prayer. Soon it is time. I pause for one more view, one more moment to seal in my memory for it is now time to go back to work. Amazing how fast the hours fly by.

It is time to reenter the reality of the workforce. The guests are coming back, and we need to relinquish ownership of the lodge. We need to travel to the valley, gather the evening meal, and start what was the morning routine now to be repeated. Summer light is fading as we finish up the evening meal and chores.

We have served the guests and completed our duties faster; dinner seems to be not as difficult as breakfast. I wonder if it is the fact we are more awake and have had our time with Mountainside.

All the extra pots and pans are in the Chevy. We are in the vehicle and are anxious to finish the day. The car coughs to life, sputters, and dies again. That is why we park it on a grade. Jump starting this vehicle is normal, and in the mountains, there is always a grade do use for this purpose.

As we travel away from Mountainside, there is a place where we can look back at the building. Lights are on in many of the rooms, smoke floats from the fireplace, and you can hear the laughter of love from the conversations as the wind carries parts of sentences across the forest. We pause for a moment, listen, look at the lights in the lodge, time to go back to valley reality. One last look says it all, lights in the rooms, but no lights in the pastoral study or kitchen.

We travel without words down to our night home. Although nothing is being spoken, this is our time of deepest communication. We silently share our unspoken thoughts as the dust of the road catches up to us. We don't mind; somehow the dust is part of the glue that keeps us together as a team. Soon we will be on paved roads, and the sealing of today's memories will be complete with a smooth road. Tomorrow we will escape again, tonight we are on to other things, but the memories of all the Mountainside yesterdays are continually sealed in our minds. Sometime, when we need those memories, the intimate thoughts of Mountainside will drift back, and we will be propelled back to that time. That is the reward for working at Mountainside, the dusty adhesive of a summer invested in serving families.

We park the old Chevy at the kitchen in about the same place as it has been all summer; this is our spot. The keys are left in the ignition. Another staff member might need it tonight, but that is doubtful as the Chevy generally starts just for us; that is what we believe, whether true or not. All the pots and pans are removed to the kitchen so they can be used again for the next meal. Our day is done. Tomorrow will come soon enough, the Chevy will be again placed into service, and the guests will be ready for another mountaintop experience. Mountainside Lodge will be ready for new memories. The lodge, the grand lady of the mountain, will be there for many more decades. Safe now as a part of the Y, loved by guests and staff equally but in different ways. Working at Mountainside Lodge is the best gift one could have for summer employment.

CHAPTER TWENTY-TWO

THE MIDNIGHT GUITAR SNEAK

Let your conversation be always full of grace, seasoned with salt, so that you may know how to answer everyone.

—*Colossians 4:6*

When you are in high school and have the opportunity to gather for a late-night summer campfire with staff, there are a few requirements that must be met for the event to be memorable.

One is to have some form of pilfered food, watermelon, ingredients for s'mores, and other forms of "good for you" desserts that are gathered at the kitchen which is closed at this time of night. With the nutrition needs being met, the next issue to address is where you will have this contraband campfire.

There are factors that need to be met here too. Security is a concern, not like you think; you must out think the evening security guards—after all, reference to the above pilfered food. No need to have to explain that.

Because the Y is rather large, there are several campfire areas that are away from the population of the guests and spying eyes of full-time staff and security. This evening we chose a site past the usual areas that was safe and we could have our time of "fellowship."

Photo of author taken close to the time of the guitar incident at Christmas in July.

At a far end of the Y is an outcropping that was created for the perfect campfire. It is secluded, and there is a fire ring where we can possibly not be discovered. Perfect. It is late at night, and most of the staff and guests are sleeping, better than perfect. The watermelon is chilled, and the campfire is ready for s'mores, excellent. But there is a hitch—nobody thought to bring a guitar.

That is where I come in. I figured I could sneak in to my room through the bedroom window, grab my guitar, and be back in a jiffy. Who cares if the time is moving toward midnight? Not a problem. Or so I thought.

The clandestine operation was put into place. Two of us would drive close to where I lived. Knowing my parents would be asleep, I would, with the skill of an intruder, slide open my window, crawl in, get my guitar, and reverse the process. Simple, direct, and fail-proof.

I slid the window open, success; then I started to crawl in, but forgot about the chair in front of the window. Have you ever tried to move a heavy wooden chair when you are partially straddling the windowsill and do it with no noise and this on a linoleum floor? The rules of physics will argue otherwise this can't be done quietly. But you attempt the process anyway. After all, you are in high school, invincible and have all the knowledge of Solomon. Nothing could go wrong.

Gravity, that is something we take for granted, until we get off balance, twisted and loose our handhold on the windowsill, which was questionable at best. I soon realized trying to move a chair by lifting it and placing it away from the window was not going to work well. I knew this as gravity and a teenage body slammed in accelerated descent to the floor, creating more noise than a raging herd of elephants.

That awoke the house. Mom, I could deal with. Dad, on the other hand, there would be some explaining to do, which was now. I didn't realize we had weapons in the house.

Here I am, on the floor, within reach of my guitar, the object of this now-questionable process, chair turned over, the culprit of the noise (wasn't my fault, or so I thought), Dad standing there in his nightshirt, Mom behind him with a stick or a bat, I don't know what. At this point I realized I may be fighting for my very existence of getting past the wonderful fulfilling teenage years. I wanted to see my twenties and beyond. That didn't look promising from my current physical position.

Looking up, I said the only thing that came to mind. "Hi, bet you are wondering what I am doing here." Silence, so I continued, "I thought I would not disturb you and get my guitar as there were these staff members who wanted me to bring it to a campfire." The illegal campfire, with pilfered food and no knowledge by any of the other staff. Good statement to make. Life as I knew it I felt was quickly coming to an end.

Dad lowered the weapon of which I was really thankful for and proof God does answer desperate prayers. Mom, the voice of reason, said, "Well, that makes perfect sense." Dad did not agree. He inquired what I was thinking, or was I thinking? I needed to consider that statement carefully; it could be my last statement on mother earth.

Truth seemed to be the best answer, but there was the issue of food that was, well, you know, pilfered, and I was sure that issue would be coming up. I considered saying I was taken hostage by staff and the only way was to get my guitar so I could be released, but I also thought that might give ideas to parents that they didn't need right now. I also thought maybe I should stand up, or at least get on my knees and beg forgiveness, neither I figured would work. I was starting to understand how much adults craved sleep, and to be woken up with a crash was not even something that was not needed.

Seeing Dad in his nightshirt brandishing a small rifle, being barefoot, Mom holding a stick, also without slippers and in a robe (she was forever dressed for any occasion) stuck me as funny.

Not the time to laugh, but laughter comes from within like sneezing. Sometimes you cannot stop it; you just have to let it go and see where it takes you. What would have been the best is if Dad slept with a nightcap. That would have been a tiny Tim moment. I started to giggle, then a little more and then laughter, nervous laughter. Dad looked puzzled, which didn't help. He was never puzzled, and the look was new to me. Mom, she started to laugh. There we were laughter on either side of a puzzled gun-bearing father.

Some things you win and don't know how or why, and you don't question it. I felt safe to stand now, no longer trying to be a small target. Again I said, "We were just having a campfire and I needed my guitar," as I picked it up and started to exit the way I came in. I figured that was the best escape route.

There are times in your life when you know your parents really understand and you realize they have unconditional love for you. This was becoming one of those moments, Mom laughing, looking at Dad, and asking if he planned to fire that antique or just put it down. Decision time, I was spared something. I don't know when, but it was suggested I exit the conventional way, through the door. Seemed a reasonable request to honor. It was also suggested to use this method from now on. Good idea, and I agreed.

I picked up my guitar, a present from Mom and Dad at Christmastime several years ago, and moved to escape as quietly as possible, lest a change in directive would be announced.

Dad shut the window, Mom put the chair back in its proper place, the process was a family teamwork moment.

Outside I looked around for my ride that was not there. Someone had turned into a chicken. I considered going back into the house and calling it an evening, but too much emotional payment was made by many to consider this option. Besides, the walk would do me good and the campfire beckoned me.

After a late-night stroll of a mile or so, I arrived back at the original destination, the campfire was glowing, embers pierced the night sky. It was good to be alive.

There was an issue: the watermelon was gone and the s'mores were down to the last of the ingredients. It didn't matter. I had one of the forbidden "chocolate, marshmallow, graham cracker" delights; it was the best s'more ever. We did sing the usual campfire songs. The one with the most meaning to me that night was a hymn of praise, "Blessed Assurance."

Never did I see the person who was my ride to the house but not back. If I had, we could have sung "Precious Memories."

CHAPTER TWENTY-THREE

THANKSGIVING AT THE Y: THE EARLY YEARS

Give thanks to the Lord, His love endues forever.
—1 Chronicles 16:34

Thanksgiving dinners at Singing Pines was also a tradition. This photo was from 1960, we would move all the furniture out of the living room, set several tables together and squeeze in for a memorable meal.

When there is a national tradition, such as Thanksgiving, family gets together, and that is the case with the Y family. We got together. I cannot recall a year that didn't go by that our family didn't travel to the staff family in Estes for Thanksgiving and many times Christmas dinner.

The camp was closed, the Ad Building was void of people, lodges were winterized, and cabins would not see any activity until late spring. Maintenance was always open, and the massive cavern of the kitchen was open on a limited basis. Because there was no groups, the only guest was the incessant wind and oftentimes blowing snow of winter, and that just passed through.

You dressed for outdoors to be indoors. Heat from the kitchen was a premium and not present in the dining room; however, the warmth of conversation was always available.

The employee dining room was a rectangular room, like a shoe box with single-pane windows that allowed light and wind to enter at will. In the summer, this eatery was filled with volumes of noise and laughter. At Thanksgiving, the room was set with many tables joined together for a family feast attended by upwards of twenty to thirty people. Full-time staff, families from Estes community, and occasionally former summer staff members would show up as they were on a break from school and away from their family.

There was little, if any, heat in the emp dining room, as it was called. So maintenance would bring in a propane construction heater, noisy as it was, to take the chill off the room. It was like a blowtorch with an attitude and was noisy and would be shut down before the meal. The heater helped, but when a room has been sitting for several months getting colder and colder, success was not immediate.

The other part of the plan was to place electric space heaters under the table and drape tablecloths to almost the floor, that way your legs and feet would have a chance of warmth. Your upper body was still in a different temperature range, well below the roasting of your legs and feet.

Big Jim was in charge of the turkey, the stuffing, and the main course of the meal. Each family would bring a salad or an appetizer. Bertha, Big Jim's wife, was the proud creator of several desserts.

One did not want for food; however, one did try to consume quickly nourishment due to the temperature range of the room. There is something to be said about Thanksgiving dinner and seeing your breath at the beginning of the meal. Perhaps that is why we all were in the kitchen waiting until the last moment to sit down.

At the appointed time, the hungry Thanksgiving crew would migrate to the dining room. Grace would be said, offering thanks for a blessed, successful summer season and the freedom of living in a country that was free. "Amen" abounded around the room. It was a family gathering of regal proportions.

The massive table was decorated with the appropriate design for Thanksgiving. A cornucopia was the centerpiece with fruit spilling out and multicolored corn decorations accented by straw flowers. What was not available in temperature warmth was present in decorations, fellowship, and an abiding love for each other, we were in so many ways a family.

The food was kept piping hot in the kitchen until the very last minute. First came the large serving bowls of vegetables. There were green beans, corn, and a mixture of vegetables. Jell-O was already on the table, no problem there of it getting warm. Of course, cranberry jelly was there. Rolls right out of the oven were served with the proper towel over them to keep in the precious heat. As the fixings of a Thanksgiving feast were presented, Big Jim would enter through the kitchen door to the dining room holding high the largest turkey he could have possibly found and cooked. It was basted to a perfect golden brown and brought a round of applause from the hungry family. Steam rose from the bird, which was ordained with decorated greens around and small paper-like hats on the turkey legs.

Big Jim would parade the main meat course all the way around the room, holding the sacrificed bird up for all to see, and set it down in its designated place of delivery on the table. With the chill of the room, the steam coming from the turkey and the ever-present coffee cups, this moment became a seared memory for all who attended.

The carving knife was picked up, a ceremonial ritual of sharpening was displayed, and Big Jim, with the skill of a surgeon, would carve the turkey. Every year the carving of the turkey was a sight to see. In a matter of minutes the gigantic thanksgiving offering was on serving platters and starting down both sides of the table. All conversation tended to cease as food was consumed. That didn't last long as there continued to be catching up to do, which was served with seconds and sometimes a third helping.

Dad would be laughing and helping to pour coffee to everyone who held the java cup up for a refill. Mom, the continual cleaner, was picking up dishes and making sure each person was taken care of and had enough to eat. I hardly recall seeing them eating, but I do recall watching these two serving the Thanksgiving staff. It was their holiday gift.

Because of the lack of television and football, conversation was the game of choice and best served with dessert. The dessert table was adorned with a variety of final food sweets. Pumpkin pie just out of the oven, cherry pie, apple pie, all timed to be just the right temperature for consumption. This was Bertha's show, and she was not to be outdone by her husband. She would roll the pies out decorated with a Thanksgiving flair, again going past people to the dessert table that until now had been void of any sustenance.

More coffee for the adults and coco for the children. Large slices of pie and, if needed, ice cream or whipped cream for the discerning tastes, which included everyone. There were dessert plates. I preferred a dinner plate.

The employee dining room that had a winter chill to it at the beginning of the meal now was enveloped in the warmth of people loving each other. It seemed as though the laughter, the conversation, and the celebration of Thanksgiving had brought the temperature to an acceptable level of living.

We could still occasionally see our breath. The wind was still blowing outside, and the rattling of the windows allowed a rogue breeze to enter the room. None of that mattered. We were a Y family; we were together celebrating a traditional holiday meal together. We were not related except by the blessing of working together as a family team.

This Thanksgiving time was a time to see the support of people caring, loving, and working together. It was a time of celebration of a family well done that was not related by blood, but by the common bond of achieving the success of teamwork.

The food consumed, the dishes washed, and the heaters out from under the table and things placed back the way they were. The room started to take on its winter chill as people headed home. Leftovers had been distributed; there was little of any dessert. Event done, memories created.

Big Jim had hung his apron and chef's hat up. Bertha her dessert section closed until Christmas. The dining room was dark, and the lights were turned off in the kitchen. The day was complete. We were nourished with not only food.

CHAPTER TWENTY-FOUR

CROSS AND COMMUNION SERVICE

*Is not the cup of thanksgiving for which we give
thanks a participation in the blood of Christ? And
is not the bread that we break a participation in the
body of Christ?*

—Corinthians 10:16

COMMUNION AND CROSS SERVICE
Dick Hall
August 21 9:00 P.M.

Prelude   Rosemary Coghlan

Call to Worship   John Lyons

Hymn: "Holy, Holy, Holy" 57

Scripture: I Corinthians 13   John Lyons

Prayer   Rev. Roger Biddel

Special Music   Marty Pearcy

The Meaning of the Crosses   Walter Ruesch

Communion Hymn: "Break Thou the Bread of Life" 216

Communion Meditation   Rev. Roger Biddel

Communion

Hymn: "Blest Be the Tie that Binds" 343

Benediction   Rev. Roger Biddel

Ushers:

Gary Nichols
Mike Bergus
Roy Nash
Ray Preston

The
COMPANION

POCKET CROSS

Program and pamphlet from the Cross and Communion Service, notice the program called it Communion and Cross service.

129

Toward the end of summer season and signaling one of the final times the staff would have the opportunity to worship together, there was a service conducted as a Y tradition to help sear the love of each staff member to each other. It was simply called the Cross and Communion Service. It was a time for the full-time staff to worship in a meaningful way with the summer staff they had the privilege of working with.

We have all gathered and worked together in various departments from different areas of the United States and several foreign countries. We were and would be bound together by the memories of a summer well worked. It was almost time to go back to college, back home, and reenter the other life we lived. That life was not on a mountaintop, not serving guests; it wasn't summiting mountains or playing cards in the rec hall. It was a far-distant life that schedules were requiring we start to return to.

The Cross and Communion service was held in Hyde Memorial Chapel, as it was called then. Sometimes the setting was church formal, other times staff comfortable, it depended on the season and the staff who were part of the planning of the service. Late in the evening was the preferred time, after the sun had set and all staff had an opportunity to attend.

Dad never missed a Cross and Communion Service; it was part of his religious DNA. I believed he saw the value of this time as the summer came to a close in bringing the staff together to have a unique, special, and memorable moment just for them. He would give out a small pocket cross that had the Greek symbols of Alpha and Omega on the horizontal member of the cross and a heart and a symbol of completeness on the vertical shaft. The cross fit with your loose change in your pocket or purse. It was a continual reminder that ultimately the money you possessed was a gift from God and to spend it wisely.

I recall seeing Dad's cross, worn and thin with his change. I imagine he carried the same cross since he scheduled the first service decades ago. Mom carried her cross in a coin purse, hers too worn as it had rubbed against her loose change.

The service would start with the quietness of a piano or organ playing a familiar hymn. Staff would have gathered outside until the doors were opened. As you entered the chapel, you knew this was going to be memorably special. This would not be ordinary, but extraordinary.

Perhaps the story at this point is best told by something I wrote after Dad's memorial service as I flew back to California.

> I carry a small silver cross in my pocket. This piece of aluminum was given to me in a Cross and Communion service at the YMCA camp I worked at for many, many years.
>
> This cross reminds me of a commitment I made to our Lord every time I reach into my pocket for change.
>
> Sometimes when my hand goes deep into my pocket, I cannot feel the cross. I panic, thinking I have lost this symbol of Jesus's love and commitment to and in my life. I grab the handful of change, pull it out of my pocket, and frantically look for this worn icon of faith. I then find it among the nickels, dimes, quarters, and my emotional panic is quelled for the moment. I know in my heart I will *never* lose the saving salvation Jesus has preserved for me; the human faithless factor simply gets in the way. Once I find my cross that my father gave to me, I calm down. You see, Dad gave these crosses out at a special staff Cross and Communion service for thirty-one years, faithfully—each summer, every summer without fail. This service, held in the quiet of a Colorado summer mountain evening, with candles, crosses, and communion, became an expected tradition for returning summer college staff.

The pocket cross at one time had four symbols. They have all but worn off my cross from time and friction of coins rubbing continually against it. The alpha and omega were embossed on the horizontal cross piece, signifying that God is the beginning and the end; a heart expressing His continuous and infinite love for us; and the monad, which is at the top of the cross, signifying a poise in nature, victory of creation over chaos, and there is a spiritual balance between heaven and earth.

Dad would faithfully read excerpts of the booklet that was given with the crosses. Each year he would communicate his feelings and his thoughts. Over the years, he showed his commitment to this service for staff and to God for God's saving grace and centered focus in his life.

I hope I have a centered focus on God and His saving grace. I hope I can allow others to see this focus. I pray for the continual commitment to God that I may give my life here on earth for His glory, not mine.

The pocket cross is a simple reminder of an eternal commitment. Keeping the cross with my spare change reminds me of the complete sacrifice Jesus gave to me. When I reach in my pocket, pull out my change to purchase something, I am reminded all that I have is His. I am reminded all that He is, is mine. It is a wonderful, fulfilling feeling. I am thankful my earthly father made the commitment, the devotion and dedication to start a tradition at a YMCA camp that has spanned decades and held my heart for over a quarter of a century. You see, the other thought I have when I dig deep in my pocket is not only of the Christian commitment, but that I am blessed with two fathers, one who raised me here on earth and the other who is in my heart raising me for eternity—each are in heaven now.

If one could transport themselves back in time, I would chose to go back to a Cross and Communion service. There I would see Chaplain Peterson giving a message about the importance of Jesus dying on the cross so we may live eternally. I would see the summer staff members dressed for the occasion sitting next to a person who has become important to them over the brief summer months. I would look at the full-time staff, once again participating in this tradition. They too seldom, if ever, missed this service. Finally, I would see Dad stand up after the solemn communion segment of the service to talk about the small metal gift that he was honored to present to each staff member. Dad presented a greater percentage of the crosses; this was his choice and honor.

He many times would take the same course in his thoughts to staff. I discovered this in a worn manila envelope he kept titled "Cross Service" after his death.

Dad would stand up looking at the staff as we would not be gathered again like this; only the Farewell Banquet would staff be together, and that was the final before the good-byes would start.

I remember there was an emotional tone to his voice not often heard as he shared his heart and his faith. Months before each person was an application, a picture, references, and a letter offering them summer employment. The staff was more than paper, and Dad was willing to share what he thought. He opened a small notepad of yellow paper, and looking around, he would say, "Can we observe God's creation all around us? The beauty of the mountains, the trees, the streams, the animals, the birds and all of us are included.

"Have you ever thought of the creation in that it is continuous, it never stops? We started out as a child, but each day of our life we grow mentally, spiritually, and physically. God watches over us as we progress. Sometimes we feel that we are on our own, but this is never true.

"We just need to take time to be silent, and in our silence, we will soon realize that God is close by, helping us with any of our problems, if we will just turn our burdens over to Him. Every step of our lives and the lives of those around us is a part of God's creation.

"The reason for giving you this cross is as a reminder to you to take time to think of the many blessings you have and to know that God is always ready to help. Use it in any way that suits you."

He would then read from the booklet that was to be given to each person. The booklet told of the story of the reason behind the pocket cross and reminded us of many human sacrifices made to ensure the religious freedom to gather together.

As Dad was the last person to speak, he would request that staff exit in silence, taking the gift of the pocket cross and not speaking until outside the confines of Hyde Memorial Chapel. This request was always honored, but feelings of finality would surface as you knew passing through the chapel doors was again one step closer to the end of summer. Many staff would be hand in hand or arm in arm, some teary-eyed, and Dad would pause with each staff member, taking a moment in time to remember them. Many of us would never see each other again on this earth; others would become family and travel back for future family vacations. All of us would not be the same; the summer had touched us as servants in the Colorado Rockies.

As the last of the staff exited, the music ended, and the candles were extinguished, the chapel felt emotionally empty, void of people. Dad would gather his notes; the others who were part of the cross service would do the same. There was a silence of a memory as the smoke from the candles filled the room. The lights were turned off, the door shut. Cross and Communion was over for another year. A few staff members would hang around for a final word with another staff member. Dad would walk alone, quietly to his car after all conversation ceased. He was alone with his thoughts, I with mine, others with theirs.

This time was the beginning of another adventure, with a cross in your pocket to remind you of a commitment with your heart.

Chapter Twenty-Five

Saying Good-bye, Forever

Blessed are those who mourn, for they will be comforted.

—Matthew 5:4

It is inevitable; tragedy will strike at the most unexpected, worst time, and you are not ready for the emotion and consequences that come with any tragedy.

Yet from the finality of life, lessons are learned, hurt subsides but never goes away, and somehow you become a stronger human being. Because of a loss, you gain.

Three deaths impacted me as I was growing up at the Y. Two staff members died in hiking accidents, and when I was a preteen I learned quickly how life can change by the word "dead" because of the stilling of a heartbeat. This is what happened as a teenage boy dealing with two people I knew, worked with, and grieved over and one young girl thrust into my life when I was much younger and not expecting to be placed in a situation beyond my maturity.

Youth program had been the same as usual, hiking crafts, sack lunch, singing, all checked off for the day. I walked home as was the case every day and came into our summer home. Mom was doing something, and I headed straight for my room, the boy cave. All that was normal, but seeing a young girl sitting in my desk chair crying was not normal and being in my room was way out of sync with the world as I knew it.

I left her there, sitting and crying, and went to the only information source I knew, Mom. "Why is there a girl in my room, and why is she crying?" Two questions that for my young mind needed immediate answers, if not sooner.

Mom looked at me. I thought she really looked tired, sad, and something else I could not exactly place. "Sit down, I need your help." She proceeded to tell me that this crying child's father was killed by a lightning strike while hiking and my dad was working with her mom to get the arrangements in place for what needed to be done in this tragic circumstance. "I am trying to get some things worked out for the family," Mom said, "and I need you to help comfort her," looking toward my room. "Can you do that for the family and your father and me?"

What did I know about comforting a girl that was, from the looks of her, older and taller than me, and what did I know about death, and death of a parent at that? This was the tall order department of life, and I had never experienced either. The look of weariness, sorrow, concern, and trust I was seeing in Mom was enough to say I would do what I could do.

The distance from the kitchen was not far enough away for what I was asked to do. I stopped at the door of my room and watched a girl child crying, lost with no direction. She had been told about her father, left alone to handle a sorrow not familiar to many children. There she sat, tears and sobs coming from her heart. I asked God to give me words to say and walked into my territory and realized territory is not important when dealing with this situation.

Kneeling next to her, I could feel the radiated pain falling off of her like water spilling over a waterfall. I became emotionally soaked just kneeling there, saying nothing. She looked at me as to inquiring what I was doing there. Reaching out, taking her shaking hand, I simply held this connection, still at a loss for words. We just locked eyes, hers in tears and mine welling up.

"Why?" she asked. "Why?" she repeated. I didn't have an answer, nothing came to mind to respond to that question. "I don't know, I wish I did, but I don't," was all I could say to this person. Her other hand covered mine and the connection strengthened. In many ways I could feel an emotional power draining from me and traveling to her. I didn't even know her name, and it seemed not to matter. We were just kids sorting out adult issues in a boy cave in the Colorado Rockies.

"I don't know what to say to you," was a statement as truthful as I could be, "but I do know I would not want to lose either of my parents. I am so, so sorry." That sounded contrite and not worthy of the sound waves that carried it. She just looked at me, tears coming and going moment by moment.

Two kids with no answers trying to figure out a fatal life lesson and not coming up with any answers.

A thought occurred to me that perhaps right now answers were not what was needed, but the touch of another human was sufficient—for now. Facts and answers would come later. The now moment was all that mattered; a presence was all that was required at this time.

There seemed to be no time frame as to how long we just sat and kneeled together, but the silence of sorrow and the presence of another was sufficient. There was a quiet knock on the post of my door. "Your mom is here," said my mother. She and I looked up, and there stood the last protector of parenthood in her life. She ran to her mom; they hugged, cried together. My role was completed. "We need to go," her mom said. "Thank you for being with Mary." I nodded, still no words.

Mary took her mom's hand, Mary waved a small good-bye, and they were gone. I looked around my room, all the same, but different. My things were still in place, but the room was different somehow. It was not just my room; it had become a safe grieving sanctuary for a brief time. A place of emotional safety and a starting place for a new journey for a family.

Walking out into the sunlight of the afternoon, I realized I had changed too. That could have been one of my parents. Then the boy tears flowed as I wondered how Mary and her family would be able to cope, but they really didn't have a choice.

I have been challenged beyond my years. I didn't say hardly anything to a grieving child. I was left with a question I could not answer at the time; how do you go home with the same amount of luggage and not the same amount of family? It would take years to supply an answer to that question.

Kim and Gary worked at the Y the summer of 1962. One worked in the kitchen, the other in maintenance. Neither completed their summer because of each died in a mountain tragedy. Both were people I knew and hung around with. Both were from the flatlands and were avid hikers and adventurers of the mountains. Every day off, they were off to summit a mountain, sometimes hiking with a group or alone (hiking alone was against the rules of common sense and employee policy). They would return with daring tales of the latest mountaintop summit. They went to different universities but were the same in adventure.

But things change, and an emotional decision can and did cause a fatal outcome as it did for both of them. Again, the math of luggage and family came into clarity.

Kim Murphy, nineteen, was from Kingfisher, Oklahoma, population then 3,249. This small town claims its fame from Chris Lofting, NFL linebacker for the Oakland Raiders, Joe Remington, the founder of the Iditarod Sled Dog Race in Alaska, and James and Sam Walton, founders of Wal-Mart. Coming from the Sooner State to the Colorado Rockies was a treat for Kim. He was a strong, strapping, healthy, and hiking kind of college student who liked to embrace the trail of life.

He was also anxious to get from one point to another, and on a hike he didn't like to be slowed down in his quest for summiting a mountain or completing a strenuous trek. Because of his anxiousness on this fateful day, Kim moved on ahead of the hiking party, a decision that would impact his life and those hiking with him.

Hiking a fourteen thousand peak is dangerous in itself and going alone increases the risk of tragedy. Kim wanted to summit Long's Peak; he didn't. There isn't a lot that was known then and now of what happened, just that he fell to his death, alone, no witnesses, and not a way to cry for help. The staff hiking party consisted of three persons; they summited Long's Peak, and they didn't see Kim at the top, as he had promised. They figured he was there, waited, and went back to the YMCA. When they arrived at the Y, he was not around, and the two of them contacted the Rocky Mountain National Park search and rescue team. That team found Kim the next morning. He had fallen to his death over one hundred feet on what the park called the cable route to the top.

Gary Noland was a twenty-year-old Iowa citizen who was wanting to experience a summer working in Colorado. He was assigned kitchen staff and was from Seymour, Iowa, population back then 1,117. It could be said Gary was a hometown boy, and a small rural town on the southernmost border of the Hawkeye State grieved with the loss of one of its own hometown boys.

Gary and three others climbed Flat Top Mountain and on the return trail passed Andrew's Glacier, an inviting, steep, dangerous snowfield that ended at Andrews Tarn, a cold-water lake. Each of the party slid down the glacier. Gary was last, lost his balance, and could not stop until he hit the rocks at the water's edge.

Both summer staff deaths happened within two weeks of each other at the near conclusion of a summer experience.

I grieved because these two deaths were a reality for a high school kid that thought he was bulletproof. The summer staff handled one death with shock and sorrow, but two deaths took an emotional toll as close to one percent of the staff was lost within fourteen days of each other.

There was a pall of sadness that descended over the staff like a curtain falling after a tragic play. This was life and death, the reality of one moment a person here and the next gone. I was working in the kitchen the day Gary died on Andrew's Glacier. The staff knew in a few short hours because he stayed with the group but chose to snow slide down the steep glacier and did not stop where intended to. The hiking party saw the incident unfold and shared what had happened. There was an emotional pall enveloping the staff. Again, another tragedy, another loss.

In the kitchen paychecks were in envelopes and placed at the end of the shelf where you could sort through and pick them up on payday. Gary died on payday. This day I had been thinking about Gary, working, laughing with him, the college student and me the high school kid. There was a hole in my soul and heart for Gary, a space that would not be filled easily and still there even now, that over half a century has gone by. I decided I needed to get my paycheck and do something, anything to cover the loss I felt, and going into the kitchen looking through the stack of checks and secure my pay was something to do at least. The stack of checks in envelopes was the largest number at the Y. Well, people had to eat and more people worked in the kitchen. The checks were always in the same place, on a shelf where you could come in and find your check. I reached up, grabbed the pile of checks, looked down, and the first one I saw was Gary's check. Seeing his name, the reality of the finality of knowing he would never, never cash what he had earned shocked me. What to do about Gary's check? I pondered this dilemma as I located my check. So I took Gary's pay. After all, I did have an inside line to the authorized signer of the paycheck, and I would take it back to my dad. I reasoned the check didn't need to be there for other people to see.

As I walked from the kitchen to my father's office, holding Gary's and my check, life seemed more precious and somewhat increasingly lonely too. One check would be cashed by the living the other, I didn't know.

As I arrived at my dad's office, I didn't greet his secretary, just went into his office. He was there, which was rare. Dad looked up. I guess he saw a look that transmitted something urgent, perhaps it was the tears welling up in my eyes, but he stopped what he was doing and asked his secretary not to disturb him. "Here," I said, thrusting Gary's check toward him. "I don't know what to do with this." I handed him Gary's check. He took it, saw the name, and I could tell the impact of the loss of a summer staff member on his heart and mind. "I don't know what to do. What do you do?" I asked.

Dad looked at me, and I could see an increase in age because of Gary's death. "I can take care of this," he replied. "Bob, this is a rough spot for all staff, and all we can do is remember the good times we had working with Gary." Somehow that helped, but just a little. "Death is not simple or easily accepted, but it is a part of life, a part of why we are who we are." The words echoed in my mind; he was talking about Gary, the guy I worked with, kidded and laughed with, Gary, always smiling. Gary, he was a summer older brother.

I looked at Dad as he looked at the final check. Dad looked up. "I know this is a hard time for you, but bringing his check here was the right thing to do, other staff didn't need to see it, they have enough to deal with. Thank you for doing that." With that remark, I wiped my eyes. He briefly placed his hand on my shoulder. We paused for a moment knowing life will continue but with a loss.

I walked out into the sunshine. I was alive; Gary was not. His family, a member short, but the summer staff and myself were filled with memories of a summer cut short for Gary and Kim, yet impacted in a positive way by the result of their lives in our lives. Perhaps that was the lesson to embrace; life is short, a heartbeat away from eternity. Here now, eternally gone. Saying what you want to say to a person is the opportunity for the moment because the moment can be taken from you, gone, done, not again. I never said to Gary or Kim how much I admired and appreciated who they were in my life. I can only do that now here, and that must be enough. There cannot be anymore.

The summer staff of 1962 placed a memorial plaque to remember Gary and Kim. This plaque can be viewed in the Gaylord Library on a book shelf end to the right as you enter. Author's photo

CHAPTER TWENTY-SIX

DELIVERING FOOD TO MOUNTAINSIDE

Whoever dwells in the shelter of the Most High will rest in the shadow of the Almighty. I will say of the Lord, "He is my refuge and my fortress, my God, in whom I trust." Surely, he will save you from the fowler's snare.

—Psalm 91

From the kitchen to Mountainside Lodge, miles of dusty roads are involved, which makes for a challenge to keep a meal decent, edible, and up to the standards required not only by the staff that prepared the meal but also the Colorado Department of Health. Well, one out of two was the best odds a person could expect when transporting food up a mountain on a dirt road.

We would do our best to cover the meal with tin foil and towels and secure the contained nutrition as well as we could. That in itself was a challenge to succeed at as the road was steep in places marked with ruts, dips, and rocks; it was a dirt mountain road after all.

There were usually four kitchen staff which occupied the front and back seats, which left the back of the station wagon, an old rickety '52 Chevy, to harbor the meal. Most of the time, the room in the back was not sufficient for what was required for the meal, and that would require storage on the laps of staff, except for the driver, although that was an option at times.

We lived on the edge of physics and gravity every trip up and back down the mountain. Brave souls that we were, we were also inventive as how to keep the meal in the best edible shape possible; we were pioneers in catering and didn't know it.

Once the food was loaded in the rear of the station wagon and on the laps of the kitchen crew, we were ready for the winding dirt road to the highest structure because of altitude on the Y grounds. The only two gears the Chevy would be comfortable in was first and second, with the default being first gear; the old straight six-cylinder engine had seen better days a decade ago.

Shifting from second to first was a grinding process. There was no syncing of those two gears, and the verbal mantra was always repeated when the gears changed, "Grind off a pound for me" or "Well, that gear was not made from Jell-O." It became a game to see if you could slip from one gear higher to a lower gear and not hear a sound. The only way was if you were almost stopped, which was not recommended as the vehicle would start to roll backward, which increased the excitement level in the car.

So you would catch the lower gear of which you should have been in in the first place, and with a jerk, the station wagon would lurch forward, and the contents of the food, if liquid or such, would catch up a split second later. The aroma of the meal, mixed with the volatile smell of gas and oil and complemented by the ambience of dust, made for more than one queasy stomach, but that was living on the dusty, mechanical edge.

Finally, the food, crew, and laughing attitudes would arrive at the lodge high on the mountain, and the meal, with the extra spices, would be served. At the end of the meal shift, we would clean up and make our way down the mountain to the main kitchen. That is another adventure mainly because gravity is not a friendly force and would try to intervene at any opportunity.

This vehicle was without the modern opportunities of power steering and power brakes. There was not a redundant system for breaking, just a strong decisive foot on the pedal and an emergency brake that was questionable. First gear was the only gear selected to the ride down. We all wanted to survive to serve another meal.

The trip home was always more quiet. We were tired and wanted to be finished with our work commitment so we could move forward with our social obligations.

Dust seemed to catch up with us more on the trip to the main kitchen, blame that fact on gravity, I figured. Slowly, with the dirt from the road leading the way, we crawled down the mountain.

We were all in our own worlds when a loud sound from the transmission that sounded like a grinding gunshot got all our attention as the '52 Chevy found new energy and started increasing in speed. For a moment, we were caught off guard, and the next moment we all knew this was not normal. The speedometer started to inch up showing an increase in speed that we did not want or need. I decided it was time to grind a pound or two or three and get this vehicle under some control. The attempt to get the car in gear was not happening; even second gear was not cooperating. I went from pushing in the clutch to cramming the brake pedal to the floorboard—nothing. And we were increasing in speed. Gravity became the enemy, and the trees on the side of the road were becoming more and more an ally of evil.

The food wagon was out of control, and we were looking at getting our lunch in a not-so-pleasant way. Again and again the attempt to catch a gear, any gear, was not happening, and pumping the brakes gave us a modicum of borrowed time. The emergency brake didn't think this was an emergency; it was just a handle pulled to its farmost resting place.

There was absolutely no conversation, only the vision of lives passing by as fast as the trees and rocks on the side of the road. Nobody considered there might be another vehicle on the road coming up; at least we all hoped not.

After multiple attempts, second gear was finally engaged much to the protest of the engine as it revved and complained about not just idling. I didn't care. It could blow up if this procedure slowed us down.

The pumping of the brakes finally had an effect, working in partnership with the complaining engine; the emergency brake still didn't care. I turned the ignition off, hoping that would also slow the vehicle down even more. You would have thought someone shot the car as it backfired time and time again.

"Guess the car ate the baked beans," someone said. We needed a laugh as the car came to a level area in the road and jerked to a halt, just about the time another car lumbered up the narrow road.

We sat emotionally stunned, pots and pans tossed in disarray, emotions frayed, and we had only traveled a few miles descending like a rock or rocket. Dust enveloped us like a blanket. We were never so happy to cough our way to cleaner air. The reliable station wagon was smoking, steaming, and smelling like mechanical death, but we were stopped.

In many ways, the car had given up its mechanical life for us. We were thankful as we walked the rest of the few miles to the kitchen.

"Where is the car?" the kitchen supervisor asked. "Dishwashing wants to get everything cleaned up." Little did they know, we knew more about surviving at this moment than many. "It is up halfway on the mountain, brakes went out, would not stay in gear," I said in my best high school maturity, voice shaking. One look at the rest of the crew by the kitchen supervisor confirmed my statement.

Maintenance was called, the brakes, including the emergency brake, were repaired, the engine "fixed," and our trusting vehicle was ready the next day for another trip.

We were too, ready to spice up the meal with dust from the mountain and a commitment to once again serve. After all, there were mouths to feed.

Often a challenge to survive a brush with death is presented in a flash of a heartbeat. Knowing what to do to avoid the finality of life is important; understanding that you might not survive is the clarity of the moment. Believing you will enter eternity because you have accepted Jesus is the calming factor, force. Because of the simple fact that you know Jesus is with you brings a level of calm needed in a crisis. I had that level of calm. Later that day we discussed our survival. Lives were altered, changed, and dedicated to more than just this world could offer.

CHAPTER TWENTY-SEVEN

SUNDAY CHURCH AND HAM DINNER

Praise the Lord. Praise the Lord, my soul. I will praise the Lord all my life; I will sing praise to my God as long as I live.

—Psalm 146

Every Sunday, there was church at Hyde Memorial Chapel. This was the ending of a family vacation and the start of the week's work for summer employees.

In the 1950s and into the 1960s the operation of camp duties and activity would cease as church started. That was signaled by the ringing of the church bell. Duke was the name of the bell, donated by Henry Dorsey and supervised by him as it was hoisted to its final duty station. Henry located the bell somewhere in East Texas in 1957.

Maintenance and housekeeping trucks would line the church parking lot, ready to get back to work as soon as church was out. The housekeeping choir was assembled and would depart soon after their presentation as the day pressed toward a three o'clock check-in that was always a challenge to meet. Sunday was housekeeping's busiest day; however, all week they had practiced for a musical presentation for church.

Kitchen crew came in to worship at the very last minute. They always sat in the back ready to bolt, lest something burn with the Sunday meal. This was the meal not to miss. The menu that was presented was the height of the week for manufactured food. Big Jim, Bertha, and the kitchen staff wanted a Sunday family meal, their culinary gift. Sometimes ham was the main course, other times, fried chicken (a recipe that traveled to Jim's final resting place and assured Mr. Sanders a place in fast-food history). Salads were fresh, vegetables somehow different, and desserts, it was good they were at the end of the serving line, with a staff member acting as the dessert police ensuring there was enough for those coming late.

I would wait for my father and mother to arrive. Mom was always early, Dad, late, nature of the job. I would hold two seats for them on the aisle midway down, on the right, as was the family tradition. Dad would come in quietly during the opening hymn. He never sang loud or a lot, but he would hold the hymnal in his gnarled hands reading the words far enough away and low enough for me to sing the words. I remember watching him as the music played. Most of the time when we were at a restaurant, in the dining hall, or the Ad Building, he was always looking around. His eyes taking in all the operations and activity. In church, that observation activity was toned down by the playing of music and listening to what was preached. He was focused, as far as I could tell, on the immediate message. I was proud to be beside him in worship. Mom always was on my other side. I look back and realize I was being tag-teamed, lest my mind and imagination stray from the present.

During the pastoral prayer, Dad was absorbed, eyes shut, head bowed. This was his moment to listen to another man of God conversing with God. I did prayer sneak peeks all the time, and this was consistent with not only Dad but Mom as well. I was never caught as it were sneaking my one-eyed observation.

Dad at some point saw the importance and value in having a chaplain on staff, and this person would bring a nondenominational message, laced with his denomination training each week. The Y had a church. The staff and summer employees were given the opportunity to worship together each week with a different, never-to-gather-again congregation from across the nation.

I realized this fact that the group now singing, praying, listening, and gathering together would only worship together once. Some families would be back the next year, summer regulars, staff, but guests would travel on to home after the service. Many cars in the parking lot were packed and ready for the trip back home. This was the final family activity, worshiping together. A fitting way to end a vacation and start a new week.

At eleven o'clock church was out, staff went back to work, and guests said good-bye to friends they had met and staff members with whom a brief vacation friendship was forged. Mom was busy taking the flowers to one of the dining rooms or to the front desk. Dad was back at work, and I was looking for any refreshments that might be had.

The piano was covered, organ locked up, and what was a sanctuary of worship would now serve duty during the week as a meeting room. There were accordion doors that would close the worship altar; they were seldom used and eventually taken down.

The room emptied faster than it filled, but souls were full with the goodness of corporate worship with people you didn't know and staff you did know.

Lunch would be ready at eleven thirty, so staff that could would hang around. The front desk crew was back at work, and maintenance had departed. Finally, the hungry group started to migrate to the staff dining room. We walked in pairs talking and laughing. Some of us were fortunate enough to work late on Sunday or were off completely.

The church bell in the bell tower that signaled the soon beginning of Sunday service was again tolled, closing the service. It would only be rung again in an emergency; it was the clarion call of need, need to worship, or need because of a situation that required an immediate response.

We walked into the staff dining room, transformed by the aroma of a Sunday dinner close to what you would have at home. This was home, home for the summer, home in our hearts, home in the height of the Colorado Rockies at a camp, conference center serving others.

After getting your Sunday meal, picking a group to eat with was the next task at hand. The senior staff would eat together. Wranglers were always relegated to tables far, far away, even on Sunday when they didn't have the aroma as much like horse evidence. Departments generally ate together. I liked to break the mold, find a new place and different staff. Sometimes I would "grace" the table of the senior staff, those of age who came and did the same job summer after summer. You can learn a lot from people in that grouping. Sometimes that was the only seat open, and the opportunity to learn and listen was offered; you just took that opening.

Bowing my head, a quick prayer was offered for an incredible meal and all the other blessings God bestowed that day and week. This was Sunday, a day of rest for most, but not for those in a resort setting that serve families coming for vacation or groups on a learning opportunity; this was a workday.

Every once and a while I would find an empty table and just watch the nourishing love envelop the room, the laughter, the conversation, the opportunity of lives being well lived.

This was Sunday, this was the Y, this was the way it should and must be, at least for me, for now. Sundays were good.

PART IV

1966–1970

CHAPTER TWENTY-EIGHT

LET'S WASH A BUS!

We ought therefore to show hospitality to such people so that we may work together.

—3 John 1:8

Vehicles get road grime when you travel, and commercial buses are no exception to this road rule. There are times one questions a decision during the execution of said decision but sees the value of the process at the end.

In the sixties I was assigned to the gas station on the Y grounds for my summer employment. Now there are a few things that were not considered in my task for the summer; I am not mechanical, working with vehicles is not in my gene pool, but filling vehicles with fuel, washing windows, giving directions, that I could do. The rest would have to be learned, including oil changes, tire changes, and all the other trappings of a working gas station.

We had service station uniforms that consisted of blue pants and shirts with our name on them as well as the brand of gas we were selling. There was a sense of unity with the staff of four or five of us that worked at the gas station. We were on our own, generally left to do what gas station attendants do. However, one summer day time slowed, and as the day wore on, time was increasingly getting longer and slower, which was a good thing for one of the staff, Dave, who saw a great advantage in kicking back in a chair and watching the world go by. I needed to do something, sweep the auto bays out of which we had two, one with a vehicle lift for oil changes and anything else that required lifting the machine toward heaven. In slow times I would arrange the cans of oil, brake fluid, and other non-environment friendly products we offered for sale. In the 1960s oil cans leaked, and the evidence was something you needed to address each day. So I succumbed to cleaning this and that, anything to keep busy, as Dave sat and would contemplate the world as it passed by, one vehicle at a time.

This particular day a large passenger bus arrived at the gas station. The bus looked like it had never been cleaned since the day it was manufactured. Dave continued to stay kicked back in his chair even though a bus in the gas station was an unusual event. As we didn't sell diesel, I knew the driver was here for another reason. Directions, I figured.

"Y'all wash buses here?" was the question. This did get Dave's attention as both of us could see a lot of work coming our way if we were the intended recipients of the question.

Dave was looking a bit concerned under his laid-back personality, knowing we were about to embark on a journey that included not only water but mud and a monolith of a mechanical monster that had more colors than dirty brown and needed to be washed. I thought what an opportunity, we can wash a bus. "Sure, we can do that," I replied. The bus driver was grinning. He was going to have a clean bus, for a bargain price.

"Hey, Dave, let's wash a bus," was my reply to the question. At this point Dave was considering being the youngest employee of a heart attack in the history of summer staff. It is interesting how people can immediately start stuttering when presented with a task they have never accomplished before that they don't want to do but realize they will be completing.

Working at the Humble gas station was always entertaining. Fuel was around 38 cents a gallon at that time. Window washing was free. Author's photo

"I don't think we should do that," was his reply. "I will pay you whatever you think you need," responded the bus driver. That remark tended to start to seal the deal and confirmed to Dave he would be part of the washing team whether he wanted to or not.

"I still don't know, that is one big bus," Dave lamented in his best Southern drawl. The bus appeared to be growing bigger before our eyes, and we had not even watered it yet.

A deal was struck, one bus wash for a specified amount. The driver left with a knowing smile that he had made a deal that was better for him than us.

"This is something we just don't do," another remark that was made. I replied we were not busy and this would pass the time quicker. "I know, but I don't care," again a remark, and my reply was, "Dave, do you know what apathy is?" His reply, "No, and I don't care." We moved on.

I figured this effort of cleaning a bus was not going to be equal, but I had charge of the water hose, whatever that meant, and the work of washing the dirt-encrusted bus would get done somehow.

We started by washing down layer upon layer of mud. Somewhere under the environmentally proper protection of dirt was a bus that needed to be shinny and clean.

Rags were soaked and placed into service. They did little to get the grime off, but we discovered straw brooms did the job and would reach the windows and higher summits of the vehicle. Wash minutes passed into hours as we started to see progress, but it was also communicated it seemed that the water was making the bus grow larger according to Dave.

Dave and I worked bucket to bucket, hand in hand, trading off serving guest vehicles as they came in for fuel. Comments were made and questions asked about what we were doing. "Washing a bus," was our proud, water-soaked reply as broom stroke after broom stroke revealed a cleaner piece of mechanical transportation.

After several hours, the task was accomplished. What was a dirty form of transportation was now a clean, sparkling shinny bus. It—as far as we were concerned—never looked better. The outside revealed the reflection of chrome and aluminum, the clarity of glass and the color of Greyhound paint.

We stood back, admiring our now labor of love. This washing of something huge was on us, and we did it and still addressed the customers who came in, the staff that needed fuel for camp vehicles. It became an entertaining point of interest, two kids washing a bus in the Rocky Mountains of Colorado.

Reflecting, we both realized something bigger had been accomplished here than just merely washing a dirty, nasty, rather large commercial bus. We had accomplished and succeeded doing something we had never done before. We had just washed a forty-foot long, twelve-foot-high, and almost eight-foot-wide bus from tire to top.

It wasn't a mountain we had climbed; others would do that. It wasn't fixing food for many or cleaning and preparing rooms for check-in. It was a large, lumbering Greyhound bus with a blue dog on the side, which wasn't there when we started.

Dave, the true Southern gentleman, stepped back, hands on his hips (I was thinking he was stretching his aching back), and continued looking at "his" bus as he now stated. There was a non-empathic pride in his look. He and I had ventured out of a comfortable cocoon of routine to accomplish a task, and we were successful.

The bus driver came back, claimed his vehicle, and told us we did excellent work and that he was sorry he could not continue to use us as we did more than he expected. He thanked us and drove off. We were not sorry we could not accommodate his wishes in the future. We just smiled and waved as he departed.

Our shift at the station was ending. The next crew was about to take over. Apparently, they didn't know what we had done as there was a lot of concern about the muddy ground where we cleansed the bus. Dave, with Southern pride, told them what we did. You could tell they were happy they were not part of our shift at the station.

As we walked to the employee dining room, each of us was dirt tired and looked like we had been through a mud bath, which we had. We got our evening meal and sat down. Dave, through some personal inspiration, stood up, went to the microphone that was used for announcements, and with all the Southern pride stated to a dining room full of summer staff, "Hey, y'all, we washed a bus today, a big bus." Staff looked at him and saw the excitement of someone who gave back more than was received. "It was fun. I will never do that again," was his final remark. Staff applauded and laughed.

This summer group was a team, and one's accomplishment was everyone's triumph.

"We washed a bus," an announcement of a then-daunting task, now a proclamation of something unique in our lives. We washed a bus, but we did much more. We grew up a small bit that day. We found out we can and could do more than we thought.

What was a simple task to a bus driver was a life growth experience to us. You should thank the bus drivers of this world. A simple request became a lesson in living for a Southerner and a Northerner working together with a bucket a broom and a hose.

CHAPTER TWENTY-NINE

ROAD TRIPS

For I know the plans I have for you," declares the
Lord, "plans to prosper you and not to harm you,
plans to give you hope and a future.
—Jeremiah 29:11

Day trips with summer staff were always started early and completed late in the same day. There were twenty-four hours in a day, and at 50 miles an hour—well, you do the math—you could go 1,200 miles. Many staff would travel great distances to briefly see a sight, such as Yellowstone National Park or Colorado's great sand dunes, and then turn back to the Y camp and call it good. With four to five licensed drivers, this was something young minds and bodies could accomplish. Gas was relatively cheap. Cars were larger with bench seats. Add the comfort of pillows, blankets, and the nutrition of sack lunches, and this made the trip a definite consideration.

What was not even thought out, or it was, is the fact one would have to go to work the next day. If you could schedule your work time to get off early the day before your day off and have a late shift when you returned, that was a bonus, but to make that work, all passengers needed to accomplish this task. That was almost impossible but was achieved many times. College staff are resourceful when a road trip is in the planning.

The information system in a working residence camp is paramount to having the best intelligence agency at your call. I sometimes think that before and during the planning stages, the rest of the staff knew about the rolling miles that would be attempted by a group of other staff.

There was the usual advice from learned travelers who had already taken that route, accurate time of travel, places for fuel, car and human, which included necessary stops. That was a relief to know and good knowledge to have available.

Swiftness of travel needed to be considered, what was the fastest route and the most direct. Staff that had trekked to the same destination were a valuable source of data and intel. The sharing knowledge of who received a speeding ticket was always fodder for conversation before, during, and after the road trip. There was always a better-than-good chance of a speeding ticket. People had to get somewhere in a hurry, and time was limited, the perfect storm for talking to the local town constable.

I never was considered a likely candidate for a passenger on these trips. I suppose being manager's son had something to do with it, and the fact I lived with the manager and his wife, that information was not authorized at that level. After all, a trip like this was edging on the tip of being outside of employee camp policy.

I saw a lot of taillights as trips began and heard the tales of the trips when the traveling employees returned. I also saw the complete exhaustion from a trip completed in twenty-four hours that should have taken three or four days.

Perhaps one of road trips with the shortest in mileage and longest in memories each summer was to the Daddy of Them All, Cheyenne Frontier Days. This was and still is the top rodeo in the nation, and cowboys from all over come to compete in the best of the best.

Getting entrance tickets is a challenge as this event sells out early, and securing a room for the night, priceless and impossible, but Y employees have a car, and sleeping slouched is a good option.

Cheyenne Wyoming is but a few hours away, so the drive is not much, but having secured general admission tickets to the rodeo, the fair, and all the exhibits requires you be in line at daybreak, and this is the summer when the sun comes up early.

To go to a rodeo also requires you dress the part; this is always interesting. Texas and Oklahoma citizens, not a problem; guys and gals from states more "southern," well, that can be an issue as the cowboy/cowgirl clothes inventory is seriously lacking. Bargaining and borrowing became a side rodeo to watch before the journey began. The biggest issue is head gear. Usually there is only one cowboy hat, no bargaining there.

The head adornment issue can be solved, but for a price at the rodeo. They sell a bunch of cowboy attire there along with a lot of "yee-haw" and "ride 'em, cowboy" lingo.

I would watch as plans were made, shifts of standing in line were assigned, and food was "borrowed" from the kitchen for the night journey, day experience, and later-than-you-should-be-up night travel back to the camp. After each rodeo, there was a concert that went into the late hours of the night. You would not want to miss that.

Getting back at sunrise was always an option and generally taken as part of the schedule.

Perhaps the rodeo was the means for something more than just seeing people unceremoniously tossed off animals, stomachs full of corn dogs and soda, and a whole day of Western activities. There was so much more to this day. As the employees started the journey to the world of cowboys and events, it was an anticipation of fun, excitement to experience something unique to the West, and a time to be with staff friends from across the United States and often from other countries.

But something interesting and exciting happened on all road trips the staff was a part of. Something difficult to explain, but was just there to accept and appreciate. There was a melting of personalities, a mixing of love in these journeys. What started out as fun—that ingredient never left—but the bonus of a traveled friendship, a lifetime memory created was the unexpected part of the trip.

Someone would purchase the cowboy hat for someone else, and years, decades later that person would still have that gift. A memory of a life event.

I have a Bible that an employee purchased for me between summers when they went to the American University in Beirut. It is part of my heart collection.

Here is another caveat of summers at the YMCA. There were hikes, trips, pizza parties, mini golf events. But if you looked and observed carefully, you would see the progress of a friendship move toward something greater than summer memories, greater than working together for just a summer.

Occasionally the road trip brought a higher level to a relationship. It gave the opportunity for two traveling souls to consider and accept the decision that the road journey should be a lifetime journey of a commitment of marriage.

There would be a change in demeanor between a couple who before were "just friends" to being more than friends. The others in the car would sense that too and would see the progressive commitment even in that short travel time.

By the end of the summer, the trips, the hikes, staff parties were now a part of a memorable history. Yet relationships continue past summertime, through the seasons of living. Some staff married the one they met at the Y; others would keep in touch through Christmas letters, reunions at the Y, and the occasional phone call.

Road trips became life journeys for many. Perhaps windshield time was the ingredient to bring to focus summerlong and lifelong friendships and commitments, I don't know. What I do know is there was always a greater part to the story you didn't realize at the time of the road trip, but reflecting back, you see in greater clarity how God brought a group of college students together to serve others and molded a group of travelers in a vehicle into a deeper friendship with probable bonus of a lifetime commitment.

After a road trip, the participants would arrive at work, get through the workday, and then one would not see any of them for the next several hours, until it was time to report to work. They were sound asleep, sealing the memories of a trip well-traveled.

CHAPTER THIRTY

A TRAIL RIDGE SUNRISE

The whole earth is filled with awe at your wonders;
where morning dawns, where evening fades, you
call forth songs of joy.

—Psalm 65:8

Sunrises have never been a college student's thing, unless you are arriving home after an all-night of studying or other college activities of sorts.

However, a sunrise from the top of the world twelve thousand plus feet above sea level and around twenty-five degrees colder than being at the Y, well, who would not want to experience this visual emotion.

Dad had located a two-door 1951 Ford that his secretary had sold. He purchased it for my travels to and from college for $150. I didn't know I needed a car at the start of my sophomore year of college. I guess they figured I could drive there, or they could drive me to Sioux Falls, South Dakota. It was more efficient and cost worthy for me to drive.

Having the car generated requests for transportation from somewhere to somewhere else and back again. Your popularity was elevated by a simple set of keys, an engine, and wheels. Such was the case one day when two staff members asked if I was interested in seeing a Trail Ridge Sunrise. It wasn't until the offer of paid gas and breakfast at a restaurant in Estes was thrown into the mix. The puppy-eyed look of "please" from a woman from the South will change the mind and attitude of any male. I agreed, which required getting up in the dark at some not necessary hour to complete the drive to a good viewing point.

On the appointed day, I picked up the two dawn travelers, and we started our ascent to the heights of the Rockies to see an orb ninety-two million plus miles away from earth that would grace us with its glowing presence. Who could not appreciate such an opportunity, we all reasoned and agreed.

The morning was cold, summer was winding down, and fall was hinting that the icy fingers of winter would soon also follow. There were few clouds in the sky and several coats and blankets in the car. We would arrive early, find a "soft" rock, and face east, shivering and waiting for the sun to lighten our day.

We drove into the darkness, headlights showing the way on a deserted road that later in the daylight would be bumper to bumper of people loving nature from the comfort of their automobile. We were night travelers expecting to open the day.

The further in elevation we drove, the colder the temperature; it was good to have blankets and jackets. The three of us hoped the supply was sufficient as we departed way too early and would be arriving with lots of time to spare.

There is a place called the Rock Cut close to the top of Trail Ridge. The road curves through this man-made cut, the road slicing a path for vehicles to continue the journey. Each of the passengers had decided or succumbed to the opportunity to sleep. I also had nodded off just before this massive rock cut in the road. I woke up in the last second before impact of car and rock. My foot had become lighter on the gas pedal as my eyes became heavy and took a break from seeing. The car had slowed down. I jerked my head up and watched the rock wall approach. That sight of car and rock joining was the alert for me to steer to the center of the deserted road and travel through the cut unharmed, alive, shaken, and now fully awake.

Because the car abruptly changed direction the passengers were jostled from their slumber. We all realized what had just happened as we steered clear of injury and perhaps death. Sleep would not be an issue for now; the parking lot was in view. We didn't have any problem finding a parking place; we were the only vehicle.

The sunrise now took on a greater depth of meaning. Nervous conversations were started, and thankfulness was recognized. I firmly believe God woke me up not only from a brief nap while driving but in many other ways too.

Our destination to watch the world awake was up a trail that, for now, was cloaked in darkness. We grabbed the blankets, donned our jackets, and walked into the decreasing darkness to a place where we could all sit huddled together and watch the opening of the day. Words were not needed here. Evidence of breathing was present as we could see the chill of vapors of our breath. We sat close to each other, shoulder touching shoulder, lives intertwined at twelve thousand feet.

The wait was shorter than expected as the sky's darkness rolled back with the anticipated light of a dawn close at hand. First the few clouds in the sky announced the impeding dawn with a change of color as the sky accented the clouds turning from an inky dark, dispersing the stars, to a silky gray. With each moment colors changed as light appeared, rolling back the night.

We could see each other now, no need for flashlights, but a need for blankets, yet the warmth of friends participating in the same experience seemed to push back the cold, just as the sun was shoving the night away.

As the eastern horizon became alive with shades of pink, gray, the sky started to take on a shade of morning blue. Not to be outdone, the clouds turned into a fiery red accented by a deepening blue sky. Shafts of God's light penetrated the darkness with their personal proclamation that morning was just under the horizon. Then in a flash of a moment the uppermost tip of the sun appeared, announcing the day. Within a moment of time, shadows of light and dark appeared across the rocks and tundra where we were.

There was silence between us as God announced in visual detail the beginning of the day. We simply watched, sat there in awe of a created day by the one who was not created but became. Sometime between dark and light we had found each other's hands; we were separate in thought but locked into a memory of a summer sunrise high on the mountain, seeing first light.

The crests of the majestic Rockies caught the morning light, and the valley below continued to slumber for a few minutes more. Morning light would fill in the valley soon enough, but for now, we had the sunrise light against our faces. It was our world, our time to appreciate being here in the moment of a new day.

The world seemed smaller and larger at the same time this sunrise moment. Shadows that were present a few minutes ago were now disappearing by the split second. The three of us sat a few minutes more as the sun grew larger. The clouds gave away their colors for a Colorado white which accented the crystal blue sky of the Mile-High State. We were over two miles high physically. Emotionally we orbited the earth, if not the universe. It was a sunrise of godly proportions.

We gathered our blankets and walked back to the car. The descending trip seemed faster than before. We continued to look back, but the sunrise was now the morning light and the day had started. We had been the only car in the parking lot. There were a few other vehicles and people now, invasion of our parking territory.

As we traveled back to the Y camp we passed through the rock cut and stopped on the road, looking at what could have been, remembering what we experienced a few miles up the road. No words were offered, or needed; we were alive, and life took on a profound depth of meaning because of a sunrise and the simple fact of just about not seeing what we had set out to observe. The rock cut was awash with sunlight, accenting the solid beauty of a massive structure crafted also by God.

Once we were back at the camp, we walked into the dining room for breakfast. We were close to the first in line, and that was appropriate. We had been first in line to witness the dawning of a new day. Somehow breakfast with a room of strangers in a restaurant was not an option, but sharing a morning meal with people you worked with was a much better idea. It was a day almost not lived, but now being able to experience with an application of God's protection, grace, and beauty.

Our lives had been changed because of a simple decision to watch the day awake, but God had a deeper plan to create an object lesson to show us the passion of life in a sunrise and to present in our souls the appreciation of His protection of our lives.

The day had begun, for us two miles up on a rocky ridge in a national park watching the sunrise. It was going to turn out to be a glorious day.

CHAPTER THIRTY-ONE

CREEKSIDE THOUGHTS

Be still, and know that I am God; I will be exalted
among the nations, I will be exalted in the earth.
—Psalm 46:10

There are two creeks that feed into the Big Thompson River, Aspen Brook and Glacier Creek. I would on many occasions find my wanderings by the shore of one of these mountain tributaries which defined the borders of the YMCA in many places. They were the natural announcement of a man-made boundary.

There is everything about the churning of glacier fed mountain water cascading over the river rocks that brings a person to a heartfelt quiet time. A time to simply sit, listen, observe, and be still in the tranquil sound of nature.

My journeys to a creek or river were seldom planned. They came about because of an emotional trigger being pulled inside my soul. A need to seek counsel beyond earth or human, a desire to open a young child's heart and as time passed an older man's time with memories past and current thoughts.

One such visit to the creek side was after a long, frustrating day serving a loud, demanding group that departed the dining room, leaving it in absolute disarray. It would take us longer than usual to clean up and set for the next meal. Yet that was our job, like it or not. Right now, we didn't like it in any way. After the task of serving, cleaning, setting, and preparing the room for the next meal, we were released with a few hours to spare before we repeated the task once again.

I wandered with not a lot of thoughts as to where I was going and discovered I was by the Big Thompson River. A river thundering with liquid authority of noise, speed, and a lot of visual awesomeness. The afternoon sun was beating down, working hard to dispel the shadows of the trees and not succeeding. There is always a place to sit where the mountain water churns its course as it travels to a lower destination.

Sitting closer to the river meant more river noise, perhaps a cooler temperature as the water spray was present. Farther away gave the opportunity to mix the other sounds of the world together. I chose to allow the river to be the consistent sound in my world at that moment. I could reach down, touch the calm swirling water, but only a few feet away the cold liquid sped past, tumbling over, around and flowing under rocks, over boulders, and across fallen tree trunks and branches.

Calm water, close to shore; not so calm water, farther out. Rocks rounded smooth by the friction of consistent water washing over them removing the harsh corners. Right now, I needed some emotional unforgiving corners removed. I was frustrated at the messy group that as far as I was convinced had no knowledge of neatness and no education as to the use of dining utensils. This was the first meal we had served them and there were going to be many more—oh, joy.

Looking at the churning action of the river, one can see different things that the river offers. One thing is the consistency of the water traveling that was something to contemplate. Each spring the waters rise, and as summer progresses, the volume, speed, and nature of the tributary change. I focused on a spot in the middle of the river where a tree branch refused to be flushed out and rushed further downstream. Restlessly the water pushed against this defiant branch; consistent was the pressure which was displayed in the quivering of the branch above the water. As relentless as the water was, so was the branch.

Other objects you could tell had been dislodged, but this branch, determined as it was, continued to hold its tentative ground. I picked up a small rock and tossed it in the river. In an instant when the rock hit the water, it disappeared. Nothing to show where it had been on the ground or in the river. I tossed another and another; all the result would be the same.

The fragility of life can be that way too, I thought. We are tossed from one rocky emotional shore to another, and like the branch holding its own, we have a choice to disappear with the flow, hold our own, and have a determination in our destiny.

I sat for another hour listening to the thundering of water over rocks, watching the wind move the branches of the trees and the shadows take up residence as the sun moved across the ground.

Resting and being in the quiet of the river as it did its continual dance refreshed me and my perspective and attitude. Sometimes it is just good to let the wears of the day go, allow them to travel down the river, if you will. Like the rock tossed into the current, if that was the frustration, the emotion is gone.

I walked back to the dining room ready for another messy opportunity to serve. "Did you hear what happened?" one of the dining room staff asked. "The leader of the group heard what the kids had done to the dining room, and, well, let's say, I bet dinner will be better and cleaner." Good news, I thought, but we will wait and see.

Dinner was not what lunch had been in terms of a mess, manners, or other methods. The group was respectful. "Please" and "thank you" were part of the vocabulary. Setting the dining room for breakfast was a simple chore.

My thin faith in mankind, restored. My time watching, listening, and relaxing by the river, no amount of money could have paid for that space in time to just be in the arms of God's river and forest creation.

There were many more times I would visit the sanctuary of a river, stream, or body of water. Each time I would feel the emotions of frustration, concern, sorrow, I would start to relax and power down, then the comfort of God's love fill my soul. Moving bodies of water do that to you. All you have to do is move to the river, sit, listen, relax, and the world will start to realign.

CHAPTER THIRTY-TWO

LEARNING HOW TO BE IN THE WARMTH OF THE SHADOW

Fathers, do not exasperate your children; instead, bring them up in the training and instruction of the Lord.

—Ephesians 6:4

Being raised by a father whose main goal is to provide a place for groups, staff, and families to grow in Christian faith and personal fellowship was an experience unique to few.

After several years of being away working at another YMCA on the West Coast, I traveled back in the summer to Estes Park Center to visit and catch up on what was happening in a place where I had spent all the summers of my growing years.

One place and person I sought was head of food service, Gary Van Horn. We had worked, discussed, misunderstood, and teamed up together at Snow Mountain Ranch for several years until Gary was promoted to food service director at Estes Park. He eventually went on to be the managing director.

I enjoyed looking up to Gary as our association went back over a decade and a half at that time. We were part of the first staff at Snow Mountain Ranch and lived next to each other for many years.

"Want a cheeseburger?" Gary asked as he slapped a burger on the grill. He knows the answer to that question. After the burger was ready with fries, we sat down at the kitchen staff table, a place where Gary and other staff could watch the operation of the preparation of meals.

We shared several not-newsworthy stories and got caught up, me eating a custom cheeseburger and Gary drinking his ever-present cup of coffee. As we talked and reminisced about my dad, Snow Mountain Ranch, about now, Gary took an emotional step back. Placing his coffee cup down, he paused, looked at me with an expression of reflection, and said, "You never had it easy at Snow Mountain Ranch. Any idea you had was not counted as contributing to the operation." I waited. Gary wasn't finished with what he wanted to say. If he had stopped there, that would have been fine because that statement he just said was healing. He went on, "Your dad ran a benevolent dictatorship, but you were manager's son, and that was a tough position to be in." With that he picked up his coffee cup, said he needed to go, and was off.

The staff kitchen table was mine alone. I sat a few minutes reflecting on the statements Gary had made. It is said words can tear apart or mend together; his words were the latter, a mending statement.

I had been raised, worked under, been disciplined, and congratulated by a person looked up to, respected, sometimes feared, and always loved by staff. His shadow towered over me. I learned to operate under the shadow of a father who oftentimes was absent because of business. I learned to fill in the blanks of family and, through God's grace, understood what he was accomplishing was because he loved family and wanted others to know that love.

That goal and desire came with a price. Dad was absent a lot, and when he was present, he was sometimes gone or lost in thought.

Measuring up as a child and then as an adult expecting to know and reflect the same expertise as your father doesn't happen. Powerful manager are just that, powerful. There is a difference in how a person uses authority. Some direct with an iron fist, "my way or highway" model of management.

Dad was much of the time at the opposite end of that spectrum. He didn't want credit for an idea; that was not important to him as much as the task being completed. He operated in a sense of a background philosophy of management. It would be his idea for a task, but the rest of the staff were given the authority to make it happen. He was always a phone call away, or a knock on his office door.

When Dad would take the occasional meal break, he would grab a cup of coffee and sit down at one of the dining room tables. I could not figure that non-nutritional reasoning for many years. What Dad was doing was making himself available to all staff at mealtimes. Here was your chance to talk to Walt. It would not take long for the table to fill, and a conversational meeting would be held.

His shadow extended across three decades building a seasonal "camp" into a year-round world-class resort, to become the largest YMCA in the world. He paid for that accomplishment with the price with heart attacks, multiple ulcers, and stopping a careening car from going over a cliff. He drove horses from summer pasture to winter pasture and walked funny for a few days afterward.

Plumbing was not his expertise, but he figured a way to do what was needed, along with electrical and other construction issues. He could flip a pancake and create an outdoor trail ride meal while talking to a potential group leader or cabin donor.

He wasn't a management superhero; he was simply part of the workforce. He just also happened to have an office that he didn't stay in a lot. The only time I really saw him in the office for an extended period was in the winter in the Denver office.

In the winter months, he would bring a large pile of applications home looking to hire the best of the best for the best, the guests at the Y.

I would watch him read every word on the application, the references, and place them in selected groups, housekeeping, maintenance, youth program, kitchen, and the "maybe" pile. This winter's evening home routine went on for many weeks; generally it was a two-briefcase project.

Over the years watching Dad, I learned a lot of management skills. He did not sit down and discuss many of his techniques with me, unless I asked. I simply was a part of the process, and some parts of the management philosophy soaked into my way of managing. I am thankful it did. I wish there was more.

Dad cast a long, tall shadow that decades later one can still see, although as the years continue to grow away from his time, you see less and less of his shadow. Others now are creating their legacy. Then something happens, and I have heard that someone, generally the dwindling old guard, will muse, "What would Walt have done?"

One of a few photos of my parents together and smiling. This is my favorite. They had moved back to their first home in Denver and had also just retired. This was at the end of moving day. Author's photo

In looking back, he was not only a benevolent dictator, as Gary said, but he was also an honest dictator too. You knew just where you stood or needed to stand with him. You were part of the whole operation, not compartmentalized with little or no working knowledge of other departments. Thoughts, views, feelings were shared, department to department and people to people.

Mistakes and accidents happened, they were resolved, and life continued. Dad used to say, "There are not problems, only opportunities." Looking back, when money was tight, groups would cancel, something expensive needed repaired, Dad saw the opportunity, and the problem was solved.

At his last farewell board meeting, he stood behind a large podium that said Water G. Ruesch Auditorium and said his good-byes. Mom was close at hand. Accolades of embarrassing praise was piled on, and I could see all Dad wanted to do was move away from the spotlight and leave quietly before the tear I saw in his eye was discovered.

The baton had been handed over to another. They could create their own shadow, but would have to step out of the one present.

I would move on to another opportunity eventually coming back to live in Colorado. Dad would travel some in retirement, but not enough. He didn't fly; he drove. He consulted on the East Coast and with me on the West Coast.

The manager at Snow Mountain Ranch, Jerry Donner, said that Dad would call once and a while and ask if the ranch could afford a hamburger for a retired YMCA executive. Dad would arrive in time for lunch with Jerry and a few other staff, again looking around at the operation, but as Jerry said, "Unless you asked his opinion or for direction, he didn't volunteer it. He was a manager's manager and let you run the show."

Dad realized he was not in charge. There was an emotional hole there that was never filled. Over the next half of a decade he simply slowed down and stopped one day, taking a final trip to the hospital with a heart attack.

True to his style, he called 911and waited outside his first house he purchased in Denver and now retirement house. When the ambulance arrived, he wondered what kept them, and he posed the question to the crew. I am sure he was wondering if there was a way to create a better response time and service.

That was his last walk. He walked away from a devoted thirty-year career into an ambulance and several days later climbed the stairway to heaven. The shadow became part of the YMCA of the Rockies history books.

PART V

DEVOTIONS

CHAPTER THIRTY-THREE

TRIBUTE

A wise son heeds his father's instruction.
                                    —Proverbs 13:1

"For I know the plans I have for you," declares the
LORD, "plans to prosper you and not to harm you,
plans to give you hope and a future."
                                    —Jeremiah 29:11

Note: Walter G. Ruesch died on April 19, 1986, after a battle with a
failing heart. I had taken Mom back home, came back to the hospital,
and he was gone. My last act of service for him was to give him some
water as he waited for surgery for a pacemaker. He now walks beside the
eternal living water. Below are the words I penned on the flight back to
the West Coast after his memorial service.

Not many photographs have Walt sitting at his desk and posing for a photograph. His work was outside the office, talking to guests and staff. Notice the organization, calendar, notepad, stapler, pencils, all ready for use and reference.

We have spent my whole life together. In that time so much has gone on. You were always there to hold my emotional hand and were there to say, "Try it on your own," when I thought I needed your help but you knew I did not because I could succeed. Yet you were there watching like a spotter for a gymnast, ready to catch me if I was to fall.

So many times, you were at work doing what you thought best and I would wait, sometimes not so patiently, for you as you finished your twelve- to sixteen-hour day. But you were there . . . always in love and spirit.

I never realized until later in my life how much you really loved me. I always thought I could never achieve the level of excellence I felt you demanded of me.

Sometimes, you said I could be better and I could achieve more than I felt I could do. Now, I know it was your way of seeking the best that you saw was in me and within my grasp. This direction would allow us both to be proud of each other through our own accomplishments.

You were, are, my support, my counsel, my understanding father.

Know that I was always proud of you and what you achieved. For your accomplishments are not measured in buildings and balance sheets (although both are impressive), but your greatest achievements are reflected in people's lives and the way you cared about each and every one you meet. Your gentle and oftentimes firm ways allowed everyone you came in contact with to appreciate their own self-worth and to discover an excitement about themselves.

You gave me many values to live by, but perhaps the two greatest values are that you taught me about a greater being than all of mankind; you taught me about God and that God can supply you with all your needs if you allow this to happen and trust in Him. The other value you taught me allows me the opportunity to discover more of me each day. That the knowledge that each person is special in a unique and exciting way. The way you learn to love them allows them to love you and, in return, also to love yourself. These values that you gave me have allowed me to also love you as a son. Even now in your death, I love you deeply, with no remorse of things left unsaid or things left misunderstood. These feelings allow me to share my love with others each and every promising new and bright day.

Thank you for being my father. Thanks for choosing me to be your son.

CHAPTER THIRTY-FOUR

THE GRANDFATHER CLOCK

There is something about the sound of a grandfather clock chiming on the hour and reminding you of the quarter hour between; when the clock stops, the sound of time ceases and the silence of time remains. Hushed becomes the quiet of time.

Recently we were at our friend's house; they have a grandfather clock that has been silent for more than a decade. That bothered me. It bothered me because the clock, simply, was not designed to be silent, but there it stood, regal, handmade by Charlene's grandfather, one of a pair for each sister, silent.

When we took a good look at the clock, we could see the polished pride of a grandfather's love for his kin. We could see the work of making the structure not only beautiful, but strong, sturdy, and in many ways, stately. Only one thing was wrong: the heart of the clock, the reason for its being, didn't run. There was no tick, no tock, no chimes, just a silent piece of beautiful wood taking up wall space with no functionality. Pretty as the grandfather clock was, it didn't have a purpose except to say, "Well, my grandfather made it for me, but it isn't working now, it did at one time, but not now."

That got me wondering if Charlene's husband and I—for her birthday and their anniversary—could get it running.

The clock had been moved from Texas to Colorado and back to Texas again, so it should have run! After all, it ran in Texas before all the moves. Curt and I took the back off, attached the chains, hung the weights, set the pendulum, and started swinging it! To our surprise, the clock started ticking, tick, tock over and over again. The hands moved, and the chimes chimed. We were really proud of ourselves, until it stopped after less than five minutes. Darn, we thought we had it solved.

We tried everything, leveling the structure, gently blowing the dust out of the clockworks, making sure the chains were on right and not hanging up. Nothing worked. It seemed the heart of the clock just was not going to run more than five to seven minutes. By the way, the chimes and gongs sounded great when it worked.

Finally, we tried one other thing. We checked to see if the clockworks were level; they were not! After several tries, we had the mechanism level. Again, we swung the pendulum. Tick, tock, tick, tock—the clock sounded different. The sound of the ticking was more solid, more even, more in rhythm that it had ever been, and it ran, ran for ten minutes, then twenty, then thirty. Two hours later, still running, and it is still running!

What was the difference? A simple theological concept. When your heart is right (level) with God, you are in sync (in time) with His will. When you are not level with God, you run sometimes, and then quit. Then your pendulum of commitment has to be pushed to start again, and again.

Like Charlene's clock her grandfather made for her, we need to level with God, confess our sins, lay our cares and concerns at His altar. Then, and only then, do we find our heart, like the grandfather clock ticks on and on and on and on, because we are level with Him.

Oh, and when we confess our sorrows, concerns, and cares, it is like the clock. He takes them and allows us to continue running. When we don't do that, the weight of our burdens causes us not to run. We simply stop until we lift our heavy weight and give it to him.

Now the house sounds with the passing of time every fifteen minutes, chimes every hour. Our lives can be ringing out the joy, blessings, grace, and a clarion call of time passing before our Lord comes to claim His church, and we will run for eternity.

CHAPTER THIRTY-FIVE

WORD THOUGHTS

Growing up at a Christian camp and meeting families and people from all over the USA and the world was a blessing that I didn't realize until much later in life, and that was OK because my heart was open to receive incredible life experiences from those whom I met, and that was almost everyone who came to the Y.

I assumed all kids grew up like I did, going away for the summer, avoiding the heat of the Denver metro area, seeing population changes each week, watching conference groups of all ages come and go; that was normal for me. I didn't know anything else.

People were people, some were adults, others college students, still others, my age. I learned to cope with consistent change. One week the camp would be inundated with athletes from across the country, the next week medical doctors, and the week after that a national youth group would take over. There were adjustments to everyone's schedule; to me that was just a way of life.

Sometimes I would watch as a horde of square dancers would dance the night away. Other nights there was a talent show; every Friday, a movie in what was called Assembly Hall, now Hyde Chapel. I learned something each day about how life was not routine but a series of surprising changes, some negative, others positive. Sundays there was always church and the best meal of the week prepared by Big Jim and Bertha. You didn't mind standing in line that day for your meal.

In the mid-1950s, I watched world-class athletes with the newly formed Fellowship of Christian Athletes as they would share their faith, their triumphs, and their losses and failures. I marveled at watching up-and-coming Christian musicians show the height of their talent to an audience of two thousand and then at mealtimes and other encounters would sit and converse with a new upcoming, hopeful talent and give in a moment a lifetime of guidance for another's musical career.

Some days I would be invited to travel to a destination with a family I just met a few days before. Trail Ridge was always at the top of their list, and Grand Lake was a bonus destination on the Western Slope. The family was instantly trusted; it was a different world then.

There were days I would play checkers with a lawyer/professor that taught law in England at Leeds University. I suspect he would let me almost win and then would slam the door closed. It wasn't the checkers game but the conversation about many various subjects that was really the game being played.

I write all this because that child growing up in a vacation world filled with reality was a gift that could never be measured in terms of money, prestige, or any other way. This gift was even more special because of a birth mom that knew she could not raise me and protect me. It was one or the other, and she took the second choice. I thank her for a decision in 1946 that was unpopular, unforgiving from society and I know heart-wrenching for her. We talked about that fifty years later.

Because of her qualified and deep, deep love, I had a life like no other, and my adoptive mom and dad, Water and Alice Ruesch, had the opportunity to bring a child into their relationship when they were older, established, and looking for someone little to love, nurture, and raise. That was God's cue to arrange a life for a baby in a hospital for the first eight months of his life to be given to a couple choosing and wanting a child.

The adoption was never a secret to Mom, Dad, and myself. I was adopted; it was simply a fact of life in our family, never hidden, just there.

So you take all the ingredients of being raised in the Colorado Rockies, meeting and interacting with students from seventh grade on, dining with conference leaders and often business leaders that shaped what America was back then, mix that with a kid who knows no different life than to count the seasons of the year by who arrives and departs and you have a mix of growing up that seldom gets repeated.

All this has an impact, and that effect and my outcome was developed in a myriad of ways. One of those development routes is in the summer opportunity of living in a relaxed vacation world, which then has been translated into a desire to share not only the thoughts you have read about me growing up, but in other areas of writing. So read on, dear reader, some of the stories when I was older and away from the Y that came about. Stories that were written because of living in a vacation wonderland.

I cannot thank both sets of parents near enough, two moms, one earthly father, and one heavenly Father, for giving me and allowing me the opportunity of a lifetime.

Chapter Thirty-Six

Good Morning, Lord!

The sun was coming up, breaking the darkness of the night. Each ray was cascading warmth and an unusual brightness into the sleepy room. "Time to get up," he thought, turning over. "Well maybe another few minutes," he hoped.

He could hear the coffee pot awake with a perking sound, and then the aroma of the warm java invaded his sleepy fog with a welcome and familiar smell.

The light was intensifying, and the bed covers didn't envelop the light anymore. There was no denying the day was beginning, and it was time to welcome the day.

He slipped out of bed and shuffled toward the kitchen, following the inviting aroma of java that was waiting for him. Like a pot of liquid wake-up magic, the very process of pouring a cup started to stir him toward full consciousness. As he started to pour the coffee, he could smell the fragrance of cascading caffeine into his favorite mug. Well, there were many favorites, but for now this mug was the one. It was crafted out of clay by a potter in a faraway town he had visited. The coffee steamed and made a familiar sound as it filled the mug. It was a rewarding noise, now that the mug set upon its sole purpose of holding breakfast.

He opened the door and stepped out onto the porch, sat down in his chair, and welcomed the morning into his soul.

"Good morning, Lord. What do You have for me today?" he mused as he sipped the coffee. "What do You want me to accomplish for you?"

He read a few articles in the local paper while he sipped his morning infusion of wake-me-up. He prayed for the familiar families, the special people he knew, and the soldiers and politicians he didn't know but were on his prayer list; the paper now worn from visual and mental reflection was precious in his hands.

There is time for another cup of coffee, another few minutes of time to see the sun shine through the trees, to feel the light caress of the morning breeze. He was almost ready for the day, almost ready to see what God has in mind for him this day, the Lord's day. Almost ready, just a few more minutes, just a few more moments to remember, what was that person's name from yesterday, or was it the day before? Just a moment or more, another sip of now lukewarm coffee, another verse to read, another thought to carry to consciousness, another day to serve his Lord, another day. *Tick, tock*—he could hear the clock just past the door, by the kitchen. He heard his bride of many memories completing her final touches. He remembered countless pleasant thoughts from all the years of their marriage, the children, the challenges, the happiness, the hopes, the sorrows, and the support they continue to give to each other. "How is it I am so blessed," he reflected, "to have such a loving, caring person at my side? Thank you, Lord, for this lady, she is my earthly rock, just as you are my heavenly Father."

"Time to go," she said. "This will be another great day, just like yesterday. Good morning, Lord, what do You have for us today?" They had been saying this phrase as long as he could remember.

He took the last sip of coffee, closed his well-worn Bible (a fortieth wedding anniversary present), looked up at the sky; the sunlight was working overtime to brighten the day. He stood up, she took his hand, and the day became just a little brighter as they walked hand in hand.

"Good morning, Lord, thank You for this day. I am your servant, what will you have us do for You today?" he thought as they walked to church. Today he would bring the Word of God to those who know and do not know Him in the sermon he had prepared.

CHAPTER THIRTY-SEVEN

BETHLEHEM

Bethlehem is a town of hills, white buildings, multiculture, conflict, world religions, and Internet coffee shops.

The shop owner begins to open an almost bombproof door in anticipation of a good business day. The bulky metal shop door complains under a creaky protest; the shop takes on final preparation for business as the sun cascades across the almost empty avenues, alleys, and back pathways. As one walks the streets of the city of the destination star, there is a sense of completeness of a journey taken long ago. The close quarters of the streets bring a sense of security, if not a challenge as one is in a maze of paths, shops, and emerging history.

Traveling through the avenue of Bethlehem is like moving back in time. The streets are narrow, winding, and with little reason as to modern-day traffic issues.

People walk in this city. It is easier and safer than taking the bus, and gas for a private vehicle is expensive—even if you could find a parking space.

Doors to businesses open directly on the street; around each commercial corner is a place of living, sometimes above the store, sometimes beside, and oftentimes inside the store in the back. Children play where there is room and chance. Games of children become positioning of small adults as they enter an uncertain world of schooling, learning, and future prospect.

Buses of foreign seekers motor through the narrow crowded streets looking for the next shopping opportunity, point of historical interest, or a local restaurant.

The streets are dusty; the dust is a pumice quality that sticks to your clothes and shoes like fine powdered glue. The dust settles everywhere, on your clothes, shoes, on your skin, in your skin. When you attempt to wipe the dust and the sweat from your brow, it is only an attempt. Cars stir the pumice, and constant clouds rise and settle around you as you walk around the city of the birth of Christ. Jesus said to share His word and if it falls on deaf ears and hard hearts, to wipe the dust off your feet and move on. Bethlehem's dust stays with you, on you; it doesn't wipe off easily. Sharing, caring, and moving on isn't that simple—it is the theology of Christ's love for all of us.

Manger Square is a large expanse of converging theology. Christians travel to see the birthplace of Christ; Jews come to the square only occasionally as the Palestinians occupy this troubled sector of the city. The Greek Orthodox Church contributes to keeping the Manger church safe, secure, and coordinated. They are the keepers of the history of faith, miracles, prophecy, and peace—for now, at least.

On almost every corner there is a military presence where personnel stand watch over a fragile peace that can and will be shattered by a single pull of a trigger or lighting of an emotional fuse.

Many corners have a local food establishment or an internet café. Cell phones are abundant, and coffee is the choice liquid to discuss local and word issues.

Reminders of religious heritage are in the shops and the churches. Vendors are willing to help support your religious choice by selling you what you need or don't need.

As the sun sets, businesses close. This is a town of military opportunity, and an appointment with fate is not to be taken lightly. Again, large metal doors to the shops close with the authority of a fortress door. Many lock from the inside, securing not only store inventory but family as well.

For many years' mom would stay at Estes Park for the summer months. One year, when in her 90's we took her on the Aerial Tramway - as we were walking I turned around, pointed the camera and said "smile". Author's photo

"You know, I do think about you every day. I do rely on you," she said with a strained, unsteady voice of a person who has struggled to get to the car. "I'm in," she said as she sat down with a thunk.

I closed the door, walked around to the driver's side, and got in. Another day, one more struggle won, I thought. She was doing all she could, and I was doing all I could too. Somehow, just for today, it was enough.

CHAPTER THIRTY-NINE

THE THIEF AND THE LITTLE MAN

S horty wasn't much taller than a range fence post and some say not much smarter, at times. But Shorty was a man of honesty and honor, and on the ranch, that counted for a lot more than stature.

When Shorty came to the Lazy Bar B, he was hired as a ranch hand and given the job of cleaning the horse and cattle stalls. Not much of a job in status but one of necessity.

"I ain't much in height, but I do what is required," he would say.

Of course, the usual nicknames were always bantered when Shorty was around, Short Stack, Stump, Runt, and the like. It wasn't known where Shorty was from, and few knew his real God-given name. He was simply known as Shorty.

The owners of the ranch took more than the usual liking to Shorty, and he and the owner's children became close and fast friends. Shorty would teach the young ones to rope, ride, fish, and best of all, wonder.

"Did ya ever wonder where all them stars came from?" he would ask after an evening of dinner, coffee, and cards. (Shorty loved card games, but only when played for fun, not money or other ranch hands personal items.)

"Did ya ever wonder what made them so purtty and bright?" he would muse.

Shorty would tilt his head back and his beat-up hat would almost fall off, or you would think he would fall over by tilting back so far. And he would gaze at the night sky for the longest time.

"Ya know, a man can see on land for maybe twenty to fifty miles," he would announce, scratching his unshaved chin. "But when you look at them heavenly stars, well, they have to be a lot more than fifty miles away, and you can see them clear as kin be. Kinda makes a person wonder, don't you think?"

Shorty would ponder a few minutes longer and then amble off to the bunkhouse.

One day, during calf branding, one of the other ranch hands started asking Shorty questions about his past, where he was from, what his real name was, and if he running from something or someone.

Shorty didn't answer for a long time, as this was the type of question only asked when the inquirer was willing to challenge the person. "I reckon it isn't any of your business, and I thank you to keep your questions to yourself," Shorty rebuffed and reached for another red-hot branding iron.

As things sometimes happen, violence struck in a heartbeat, then there was one less soul.

The other ranch hand had given a serious challenge, and Shorty responded, only to see a final black powder flash as he reached for a branding iron with the same hand he would have reached for his six-shooter.

The other ranch hand thought Shorty was going to fire his gun in response to the questions, and he fired his gun first. That was it, just miscommunication, plain and simple.

Shorty slumped to the ground never to move again, cows and their offspring scattered, and other ranch hands ran to see what had happened. They had heard the sound of the gunshot.

What they found was one ranch hand, gun drawn, and Shorty dead with a branding iron in his gun hand and a lot of confusion.

They buried Shorty that same day on the range in a pauper's grave with his name on a hastily carved board. No one knew of any

195

relatives, kin, or friends. Shorty had come in with the wind and left the same way.

The only memory of Shorty was now back at the bunkhouse, a sleeping bag, some personal items, a few shirts, and saddle bag containing some papers and an old photo album.

Some of the ranch hands wanted to play cards and gamble for Shorty's meager possessions. But they remembered that Shorty didn't like gambling, so they decided to look through the saddlebag to see what was there and then give his belongings to whoever wanted or needed them.

It became unimportant who took or received what, but the contents of the saddlebag became very interesting.

Inside there were some personal papers, letters, and a photo album.

There were several letters returned unread but addressed to a Mrs. Linda Beckett and daughter, along with as photo album that contained a few tattered, faded, and worn pictures of a man much younger and much happier.

One picture in particular showed three people, a proud and smiling family man with his arm around a well-dressed woman and a small child held in Shorty's arm, perched on his hip. This was a portrait of a happier time in Shorty's life, one no one had any knowledge about. There were several other pictures in the album, with all three people involved in some family activity. But there were more blank pages than ones filled with photographs of happy people.

The ranch hands looked over the photo eulogy, passing the album around. As each person looked at the pictures of a happier time and a history captured, an envelope fell to the floor.

The writing on the envelope simply stated, "Open when I am gone. Shorty."

The handwriting on the envelope was simple, but with style. The envelope was passed from one person to another, each not wanting to be the one to find out what was contained in the envelope.

It was as if you were now challenging the past facts to come forward, and no one wanted to know anymore. Shorty was gone. He had been someone different than the ranch hand that cleaned the stables and made the children wonder about the stars. Gone was the person who wouldn't play cards for money or possessions.

It was as if his life came down to this envelope with the instructions to open at his death.

The envelope protested at the invasion of the contents being ripped from the inside. There was only one page. It said,

Dear Friend,

I call you that although I might not know you because you have found my final thoughts. Thank you for taking the time to read them.

I don't know how I died or where, and that is not important. What is important is what I lived for.

When I was a young man I was successful in business and thought I could have the whole world my way by buying what I needed. If I didn't have enough money, I would earn by sometimes honest and more than sometimes dishonest ways the money to get what I wanted.

I had a beautiful house, fine things in the house, a wife who loved me, and a little girl who was my whole world.

Those things are gone now because of my greed, my cheating, and my thievery.

I wanted it all, and I didn't realize I had it all. So I cheated on business deals, and I gambled.

That is where my life ended up, cheating in cards as well as business, and that affected my personal life. I lost my wife and child when I was caught cheating in cards. I shot a man, not dead, but a shooting is a shooting.

I went to jail for twenty years. I never saw the stars, the moon, or a sunset for all those years.

When I was released, I didn't have a wife or a child to go to. They were gone forever. My business was taken over by the very persons I had cheated in business deals.

So I traveled to wherever you are reading this letter, cowpokin' along the way to earn enough money to live on.

Please give my personal things to people who need them.

You see, I did have power back then. It was with my family, not in the money and business deals.

The power was within a person. God had given me a loving family and a wonderful daughter, and I bet it all against cheating, lying and gambling. I lost it all.

Like I said, for twenty years I never saw a sunset, the stars, or the moon. The prison guards allowed me to go outside for only an hour a day, but only during daylight.

So now, when I would look at the stars, I see two things. First is God's forgiveness and love in the twinkling of the stars, and the other is a hope somewhere my child and her mother are looking up at the same time seeing the stars or moon. Somehow it makes me feel a little closer to wherever they are.

Thank you for taking the time to read this letter. Give a way my things, and put me to a final rest. I am obliged.

One other thing I would ask of you. In your travels if you happen to cross paths with my daughter and wife, tell them I loved them to the end. Give them the album and this letter.

Tell them, well, they will know I'm gone, and that is enough said.

For you, friend, take the example of my life. Change yours. Love God. Find your family, tell them you love them, and don't go through life cheating, lying, and gambling. All it gets you is in trouble and maybe an early grave.

I am sorry for what I did, but sorrier for what my life did to the two I loved most. They need to know that.

I thank you for your time, your hospitality, and your honesty.

Shorty

The reader folded the letter, took the photo album, and placed them in the saddlebag that had been Shorty's.

He stood, adjusted his hat, and took his long coat from the rack by the door of the bunkhouse. He picked up this saddle, looked around, and said, "Well, gents, I guess I better be a-lookin' for Shorty's family, they will need to know it is over." He opened the door and walked out. It was dusk, and the first star of the evening could be seen just over the blue-and-gold horizon.

"Thanks, Shorty," he thought. "You have helped me with direction of my life, and now, I guess you will help me find the way to your family."

CHAPTER FORTY

THE OLD PEW

The old pew sits with its back against the wall, discarded and shoved aside, its usefulness now gone. The once-polished wood now is weather-beaten and worn from the timeless elements of wind, rain, snow, and temperature.

At one time the pew glistened with a striking finish of craftsmanship; the pew now is aged, still trying to hold its own from the weather as it sits quietly on a porch for a weary traveler to come and rest.

The pew that once held parishioners in celebration, reverence, song, sorrow, and praise has served its usefulness, or so it seems. The arm rails that were there to steady the worshiper as they sat down are worn from hands of time and a century of service. Hardened hands that may have bailed hay, tilled the land, healed the sick, comforted the lost touched this quiet rail, now time past.

The timeworn pew has hushed stories to share, but counseled privilege will keep the secrets safe from gossip. Perhaps secrets of joy as a family sat here seeing their child wed, secrets of a person who with unmatched sorrow finally allowed God to take the sorrow and replace the emotion with joy. There could be the undisclosed emotion of a family lying to rest their grandfather, grandmother, spouse, or a child taken by tragedy or disease at an age too young.

The pastor would have sat and kneeled here in prayer, trusting God to provide, and prayed for the congregation, the weather, the crops, the livestock, the issues of a congregation.

Weddings, funerals, dedications, sermons, quiet prayers, thundering hymns, laughter, tears, joy, and excitement happened in this old pew, a place to rest now resting with its hooked nails and screws showing. The wear of emotional ages and weather present in every crack and crevice is almost too much for this man-made object of rest to bear.

A few more years and the pew will be gone forever. Weather will have taken its final toll, but the reason and purpose for which it was built will stay in the hearts and souls of the people who have been seated here. So the pew awaits the next visitor, awaits the next opportunity to provide rest and a time to just be still and know there is a God.

CHAPTER FORTY-ONE

PRAISING GOD

How do you not praise God for all He has done? Barb and I have been across the United States seeing His work in action, His commitment and works. From churches of only a few members to worshiping in the mega works of larger congregations. We have now settled in our mountain home until the end of September.

We have witnessed His hand in saving the lost in a park in Alamo, Texas, as a ninety-year-old man accepted Jesus and went to his savior a few weeks later. We have hosted several concerts with Christian musical artists and seen the results of their gifts soften the hearts of those who know Him and those who do not know Him.

Barbara, the international servant, traveled to Mexico several times to work at a youth camp, painting, pounding, and praying for this humble youth camp to bring into focus the future leaders of Mexico as to how Jesus can turn this nation toward God. She also worked with our church services each Sunday coordinating our hymns on PowerPoint and also coordinating the slides for the sermon material. She also helped set up the sound system, and so many other tasks!

Her commitment to Him also involved working with twenty-seven pastors in thirty RV resorts for monthly meetings and other support duties. (Bob worked with the local association and also the First Baptist Church of Los Fresnos as their marketing and outreach coordinator.)

How do you *not* praise God for all He has done? You continue to sing His praises for the grace He gives you. You continue to say the constant prayer for His direction in your life, your marriage, your commitment to serve Him.

Our winter was one of content, challenge, and courage to serve Him in a unique and special way from Florida to Texas, to Washington and to Idaho; we visited churches, worshiped and praised Him for all He has done.

Thank you for your prayers. Without your commitment, our task would be much more of a challenge.

CHAPTER FORTY-TWO

GPS THINKING

What did we do before global positioning systems, or GPS? Barb and I first purchased our GPS in 2000, and today, we have several of those electronic road map marvels to work with.

We can figure our trip down to the exact route and how much fuel we may use and the cost of the journey. We can find a specific restaurant, campground, or movie theater by setting up search parameters. We type in an address, and within a few seconds—presto—the route is laid out for you down to the time you will arrive. This "cute" piece of electronic gadgetry will even talk to you, if you let it. My favorite word is "recalculating," and my not so favorite phrase is, "Make a U-turn at your earliest convenience."

However, these electronic marvels are not without some issues. Sometimes that little gadget will lead you down a road you really don't want to go on. One time we thought we would check out the route with the car. It seemed too good to be true, yup; a dirt road would have been in our future, not a good thing in an RV.

Last week our GPS quit working because of a fuse being blown. We had traveled the route home several times, should not be an issue or problem—wrong. Barb and I have come to rely on the bossy electronic whiz; we were lost without it. We—well, I turned early, got confused, and started down a road (not dirt) that was not where we wanted to go.

We could see the error of our route, did a U-turn, and got back on track. But that episode of being lost got me to thinking. We rely on our GPS for directions, places to stop, eat, and shop. It's company in our RV or car and is almost part of the family. We rely on its guidance every trip we take.

Do we rely on reading the Bible (God's GPS) every day? Do we take to heart the directions He has laid out for us on our travel trip of life? When we stop our daily devotions, our study of His word, is when we get lost in our daily grind, and I am not talking about a coffee shop.

So for Barb and myself, we will rely on the human GPS to get us to our earthly destination and God's GPS, the Bible, to get us to our eternal destination. After all, doesn't GPS mean God's Plan of Salvation? The Holy Bible will never direct you on a wrong road.

Prayer: Our Father, you are the master of direction. Please help us to consult you in all of our decisions and travels on life's path. Your will, not ours, as we venture forth in this life path. Thank you for being absolutely accurate in your direction. Amen.

CHAPTER FORTY-THREE

YOU ARE FIRED!
GOD IS FAITHFUL

"I want your keys, and you are fired." Well, that was not what I was expecting from the meeting with my supervisor of eighty-nine days, just one day shy of the end of employment probation. I knew we didn't fit corporately as well as we had both hoped, but I felt we could work out any personal and job friction and build a strong team.

Fired without notice, no warning or compassion, just turn in the building keys, get my personal things, and leave. Done, gone, finished. What would I do? How was I to survive as I was raising my daughter, and what would I say to others who would ask what happened, and the best one, "What do you do for a living?"

I left and went home feeling a dejected loss of identity, cast away like yesterday's bad news. "It will be OK," I heard somewhere down deep in my soul, but I was not feeling that way at all. "All will turn out for the best." There was that voice again. "Will you take up the cross for Me?" Now things were getting scary. No job and I was being asked to follow and trust in Jesus more than I had at any time in my life.

Jennifer, my ten-year-old child, and I have moved to a new town only four months ago. We didn't know anyone in this large metropolitan town. I had purchased our first home. I thought this was a great time to invest in a permanent domicile, and now it looked like this purchase was a bad decision. Where did the dreams and faith go that I had so willingly placed in the future and thinking of a better life for the two of us? The dreams were shattered, broken like glass that had fallen on the floor and had shattered. It could and would not be fixed, just a bunch of shards representing what was and now would be.

Shortly before we moved, I had re-enrolled in college. I was planning packing four good years of education into twenty-five years. With the current allotment of almost unlimited time on my hands, I decided I could apply more effort to my intensive studies and obtain that elusive degree I had chased and quit seeking years ago. At least this was the immediate plan; however, money for living and tuition would be a major issue. There was some savings, but not near enough. I needed to get a job. The wolf was at the door, and he was not going to knock to get in.

In a quiet moment and with a bit of apprehension, I asked God for His support as I sat and prayed in our living room. I continued to contemplate my financially completely bleak future, or so I thought. A verse came to mind from the book of Matthew talking about having enough faith to move mountains. I asked God for the beginning of that faith, a faith that would see me through this uphill part of life. There were emotional and financial mountains to climb and move, and I would need all the divine intervention and faith I could receive.

Weeks turned into months, and job interviews stacked up in number like cards in a deck. Appointment after meeting turned into rejection after rejection. I was overqualified, underqualified, I was too old, too young, didn't have enough of this or that, or something kept me out of the employment box.

My faith was strong and yet would waver at times, but the quiet thundering voice of God would continue to say with deep-seeping authority in my soul, "Things will work out for the best." Easy for Him to say; He was God. A little more help here would be more than appreciated, I thought as I saw the small amount of cash continue to disappear from our checking and savings account. Thank God for unemployment.

With dwindling finances and continuing house payments and other bills, I would be close to the last dollar and sometimes even penny, and at the precise time of need a check would arrive. My car was vandalized. I had insurance. The insurance company had a check. Immediate financial problem solved.

How often we depart from the wonderful, loving discipline of God's faithfulness in and for us. How often we try to move our mountains of uncertainty with a human shovel instead of a divine prayer. All we would need to do is ask and trust in His provision. How often we only see part of God's plan, refusing to look at the whole picture and accept by faith and trust the future already planned for us by our Savior. We long for the faithfulness of God and yet don't believe and place into practice His love, grace, and faithfulness. How much we need to know and trust Him more intimately.

Eventually we moved once again to a new town, and God's plan was revealed to me step by step. Losing my corporate idol identity was in retrospect a good thing as I regained my Christian identity.

I had asked God for His help. He said, "Don't worry." I did worry, but I didn't need to, however, because His plans were already laid out for me and for Jennifer.

I finished my education at the precise time a job offer requiring the life and educational skills I possessed was available. The right job and I was the right person at the precise time. It was God's timing, not mine.

I learned that God is always there, but many times we are not where He wants us to be. God is faithful. I will continue to be faithful, trusting, loving, honoring Him. I may waver occasionally in my faith, that is just human, but in the end, I come running back to His loving arms, and He lifts me up, places me on His lap, and I hear Him say, "Don't worry, it will be OK, I am here."

CHAPTER FORTY-FOUR

THE DAY AFTER CHRISTMAS, SKI GROUP CHECK IN AT SNOW MOUNTAIN RANCH

Offer hospitality to one another without grumbling.
—1 Peter 4:9

The snow fell silently, like white feathers from heaven. This was going to be an incessant storm, I thought. All through the night and perhaps through the next day snow is going to fall. I continued my thought, "That is what it is all about." I watched the white of winter build up higher and higher outside of my office window in Pinewood Lodge. Groups were due in; we were going to be at full occupancy, which means looking for a few more beds. This was a game we played. We would book lodging until we were full and watch the ski groups come in, saying, "We have just a few more, we hope you don't mind," as they often said.

The sky was a cold gray beating out the sun, which had not been seen most of the day. I thought, watching the gray turn darker, that this was going to be a good snowstorm.

My observation of weather lasted only a few minutes. It was time to make certain that we were ready to host the many of vacation skiers due to arrive very soon. Let's see, rooms were ready. Ellen Hay had completed her work in housekeeping. Ron Snider was busy in the kitchen preparing for the fact that some groups would arrive late and would want and need to eat—not his favorite scenario, but part of the SMR ski package. Dick Engle, camp manager, was ready to help plow with Glen Tilghman (he is the mover of dirt or snow, depending on the season). The players were in place; we were as ready as you could be.

As the flakes continued to fall, the roof was warm from the building heat, and the melted snowfall started manufacturing icicles that would grow through the night into four- or five-foot monsters. Like winter claws, the downward growth of the icicles was only halted by people snapping them off. I sometimes wonder what would happen if they could continue to grow and join the frozen the ground. Would they last until spring?

All SMR, the facilities and the staff, is ready for the continual welcoming of ski groups from places with little or no snow and no ski areas. The day was December 26, the day after Christmas, and the college and high school groups would be arriving throughout the night.

Dark were the skies, quiet is the snow, loud is the pounding of the road grader as Glen continued the vigil of moving masses of white champagne, as the ski industry called it. You could see the headlights of the grader in the swirl of the snow. The cabin guests were in their respective cabins with a fire, no doubt—families making memories for a lifetime with multigenerations gathered to celebrate Christmas, the birth of Christ, families that traveled for miles from their secure homes to be together at the Christmas season. Sometimes you could almost hear the laughter of love as they shared the experiences of the day and their lives together.

Maury Flanagan calls from the ski rental center. He doesn't really have to call. He can yell the two hundred plus yards from the ski shop and be heard and understood. This I know because I made a bet once with a group leader that Maury could, in fact, do that. I won. That is why radio personality Pete Smyth called him Foghorn Flanagan on his morning radio show.

The staff is ready, like an army waiting the invasion of territory; we are all ready to serve. College students from all walks of life and educational disciplines, full-time staff, some who just came for a summer and now are here for a career, volunteers, although few are here, and former staff members who want to work so they can ski—all are ready.

The snow continues to fall even harder now, which it often does in the evening. The pine tree branches are bending under the weight, and the few streetlights are losing the battle to shine and illuminate the parking lot, which Glen and his road grader has scrapped now for the umpteenth time.

Headlights shine through the white swirl, a bus, and then another bus. Groups start to arrive, safely traveling over Berthoud Pass, a twelve-thousand-plus-foot mountain pass, then down the mountain into what the early settlers here called Middle Park. Excited high school and college groups come from Texas, Kansas, and Nebraska to slide down the white powder of Winter Park Ski Area, only to take the lift again and slide back down again. That is the routine when you want to come to SMR and ski.

The buses park on the plowed lot, not where they are supposed to but they are parked, and from inside a warm cocoon of travel, the passengers erupt with youthful energy. "We have a few more than planned, I hope that is OK," says the group leader as we meet. (Because you are working there and you know the season and almost the date by the groups arrive.)

Now the process begins, checking in, the assignment of rooms, meal tickets, mealtimes, rules and regulations, what can be offered after skiing. The memories now are being made as the conference guests battle each other in the parking lot armed with snowballs.

Maury calls once again, "Hey, I think I heard some buses, can you send them over for their ski fitting?" Sure, Maury, just as soon as I can, I can always hope. Ron Snyder, food service manager, comes in to the office. "Do they want to eat now?" Ellen Hay, head housekeeper, follows—seems diesel engines can be heard wherever you are. "Call if you need something." She disappears as quietly as she came in. Never figured how she does that. Dick pokes his head in my office. "I will be here, let me know what you need." Then disappears into the falling snow night.

It is late now in the evening; we all have worked a massive fourteen-hour day, preparing for the groups to arrive, setting up for just this moment to create an atmosphere for memories for church groups, memories to build upon when they get back to their homes and their youth groups.

A snowball hits my window. One of the youth group gals screams in delight. The group leader senses he needs to get out there and calm things down, but forty-five to one is not a good ratio to control. He will, or at least attempt to. He will more than likely become the target of a barrage of snowballs, hopefully away from my office window.

The snow still falls quietly. The winter ski season or Christmas vacation has officially started, again—and again, for the first time.

The peaceful falling of snow has been cancelled by the human excitement of people in a winter wonderland. That is a good thing.

ABOUT THE AUTHOR

Author portrait by
Kimberly Anderson Photography

Robert N. Ruesch grew up at Estes Park Center, YMCA of the Rockies. Each summer he would have the experiences of meeting families, college staff, and conference guests from the United States and many countries.

From the 1950s through the college years, he had the opportunity to work, play, learn alongside people from many avenues of life. Unlike most children growing up, his friendships were as varied as an artist's pallet of colors, which gave him a unique perspective on the values of meaningful relationships.

Because he was the manager's son, he was known as Walt's boy. This family relationship came with many challenges and opportunities to observe and develop a life perspective living in a seasonal camp that now is a world-class resort and the largest YMCA in the world that hosts family reunions, vacations, conferences.

CPSIA information can be obtained
at www.ICGtesting.com
Printed in the USA
FSOW04n1822010717
35715FS